Professional
Development
Schools

Critical Issues in Teacher Education

American Association of Colleges for Teacher Education, Series Sponsor

AACTE

Professional Development Schools
Weighing the Evidence
Ismat Abdal-Haqq

Will Technology Really Change Education?
Practices and Promises
Robert F. McNergney, T. W. Kent

Professional Development Schools

Weighing the Evidence

Ismat Abdal-Haqq

CORWIN PRESS, INC.
A Sage Publications Company
Thousand Oaks, California

For information:

Corwin Press, Inc.
A Sage Publications Company
2455 Teller Road
Thousand Oaks, California 91320
E-mail: order@corwin.sagepub.com

SAGE Publications Ltd.
6 Bonhill Street
London EC2A 4PU
United Kingdom

SAGE Publications India Pvt. Ltd.
M-32 Market
Greater Kailash I
New Delhi 110 048 India

Printed in the United States of America

Library of Congress Cataloging-in-Publication Data

Abdal-Haqq, Ismat.
    Professional development schools : weighing the evidence / Ismat Abdal-Haqq.
        p. cm.
    Includes bibliographical references.
    ISBN 0-8039-6349-1 (acid-free paper). — ISBN 0-8039-6350-5 (pbk. : acid-free paper)
        1. Laboratory schools — United States.   2. Teachers —Training of —United States   I. Title.
    LB2154.A3A327   1997
    370'.71—dc21   97-21137

This book is printed on acid-free paper.

98 99 00 01 02 03 10 9 8 7 6 5 4 3 2 1

Production Editor: S. Marlene Head
Editorial Assistant: Kristen L. Gibson
Typesetters: William C. E. Lawrie and Laura A. Lawrie
Cover Designer: Marcia M. Rosenburg

Contents

Foreword

For 30 years I have been involved in studying, teaching, organizing, and writing about partnerships, coalitions, and networks in education. There is no question that bringing school- and university-based educators together with their communities is a powerful idea. But as history has shown us, this idea is very difficult to put into practice. Good ideas in education continue to resurface, however, precisely because their goals are worthy and we keep learning more about how to bring them to life.

Such is the case with the growing move to create professional development schools—a special case of school-university partnerships. Since the mid-1980s as part of the school reform movement, professional development schools have sought to revitalize teacher education in the university and reform K-12 schools at the same time. As part of a five-point agenda, the idea of a professional development school is to create a partnership between a given number of schools and a university; rethink the preparation of pre-service education students; provide professional development for the experienced teachers from whom novices will learn; model exemplary practices that will lead to student achievement of a high order; and provide sustained, applied inquiry for both students and faculty in both institutions.

This book provides the field with an excellent primer in how far we have gotten with this ambitious agenda and how much farther we have yet to go. Reviewing "mainstream" literature (traditional research) and "fugitive" literature (video, glimpses of practice, newsletters, etc.), Abdal-Haqq provides us with a comprehensive picture of the benefits of professional development schools: Beginning teachers appear to be more accomplished, more confident, and better equipped to take over a classroom than their traditional counterparts; professional development is more enabling and empowering; clinical experiences appear earlier and are longer and more structured; assessment strategies are part of the repertoire; school-based faculty are involved in the design and implementation of coursework; students tend to work in cohorts; and there is some evidence that they outperform traditional teacher education programs.

There are challenges too. Early evidence shows that there is more going on in these partnerships concerning preservice preparation than there is about continuous inquiry and student learning; time to learn for preservice and inservice teachers is hard to come by; financing these new partnerships has rarely been touched; technology appears to be a small part of the collaboration; integrated services, particularly in urban areas, is noticeably missing; and vision statements that contain statements about equity and diversity seem more hollow than real in changed pedagogical and organizational practices.

This book makes a significant contribution to an understanding of this important and complex reform effort. Gathering an exhaustive amount of data from numerous sources gives the reader a picture of these partnerships that no other collection has yet accomplished. But this is no mere listing of studies; rather, it is an intelligent, critical analysis of what's here, what's not, and what is missing from the conversation altogether. On balance, these partnerships are alive, growing, developing new roles, relationships, curricula, and organizational collaborations that may indeed have a chance of being institutionalized. However, they must, as Abdal-Haqq reminds us, deal with the tough problems of equity and diversity within the essence of what they purport to do; otherwise they are in danger of becoming simply more efficient replications of what we already have.

This book is a treasure chest of information for those who want to create professional development schools, those who wish to study them, and those students of school reform who want to deepen their understanding of how worthwhile—and how challenging—it is to try to change school cultures.

ANN LIEBERMAN
May, 1997

About the Author

Ismat Abdal-Haqq is a program associate with the American Association of Colleges for Teacher Education (AACTE). In 1991, she helped to establish the Clinical Schools Clearinghouse (CSC), a national center for the collection, generation, and dissemination of information and resources on professional development schools (PDSs). She serves as coordinator of CSC and the Adjunct ERIC Clearinghouse on Clinical Schools.

Abdal-Haqq also coordinates the AACTE-Metropolitan Life Institute on Culturally Responsive Practice, works with the ERIC Clearinghouse on Teaching and Teacher Education, and has served as program coordinator for the AT&T Teachers for Tomorrow program, a clinical schools demonstration program based at AACTE. She is a former classroom teacher and has taught GED classes at the University of the District of Columbia. She has been a site reviewer for a PDS partnership and reviewer for a federal professional development awards program.

She has authored a number of publications on professional development schools, including two national directories and an annotated bibliography and resource guide. Her articles on PDSs have appeared in the *Journal of Teacher Education, Contemporary Education,* and the *ERIC Review.* She has served on several task forces related to policy and practice in PDSs.

Abdal-Haqq graduated from Mount Holyoke College and received her master's degree in educational technology from Trinity College in Washington, D.C. Her research interests include professional development schools, educational technology, and culturally responsive practice. Current projects include preparing for publication a report on the AT&T Teachers for Tomorrow program, producing a new edition of CSC's annotated bibliography and resource guide, and conducting a third national survey of PDSs. She is a member of the American Educational Research Association and the Society for Technology and Teacher Education.

Introduction

The "second wave" of education reform, which swept across the United States in the mid-1980s, was stirred by two major concerns. Pragmatists feared that the country's long-held position as the world's preeminent economic power was being threatened by other nations, nations with better educated workforces. Reminiscent in some ways of the consternation many experienced in the 1950s when the Soviet Union launched its Sputnik satellite, fears about losing our economic hegemony prompted calls for more rigorous and relevant education for America's children. The other concern driving this reform movement was rooted in social justice considerations. The growing disparity between the economically advantaged and the economically disadvantaged was reflected in the widening gap between the academic achievement levels of children from these two groups.

The pragmatists—worried about the country's eroding economic position—and the social justice advocates—fearful that succeeding generations of children were destined for the welfare rolls, drug addiction, premature death, prison, or joblessness—found common ground in a belief that improved schooling could make significant headway in reversing these negative trends. Reformers from both camps saw better schools and better teachers as crucial to America's social and economic well-being. This climate gave birth to the school restructuring movement and to the movement to redesign teacher education to better prepare teachers for restructured schools. (See Lange [1993], Shive [1997], and Hecht et al. [1996] for discussions of various reform movements and the historical context that spawned professional development schools.)

Professional development schools (PDSs) emerged in the mid-1980s as a potentially significant vehicle for advancing both the revitalization of teacher education and the reform of P-12 schooling. They were advocated in several influential reform reports and studies of the era (Carnegie Forum, 1986; Goodlad, 1990; Holmes Group, 1986). Because PDSs would be designed and implemented by school-college partnerships, they were envisioned as institutional settings that would be both models of best P-12 practice and optimum sites for clinical preparation of novice teachers. In addition, they were to be schools where new knowledge and organizational structures could be generated, tested, and refined. The practices that emerged from these schools could then be disseminated to the larger education community. Their role was frequently compared to that of teaching hospitals in exemplifying the best in medical practice and providing rigorous, systematic, coherent training for new entrants into the profession. Under various labels—professional development school, professional practice school, clinical school, partner school, professional development center—the concept captured the imagination of educators, legislators, policymakers, researchers, journalists, and funders (Clark, 1995).

Over the last decade, more than 600 individual public and private schools have been designated as PDSs, partner schools, etc. (Abdal-Haqq, 1996a). Data collected in 1993 by the American Association of Colleges for Teacher Education (AACTE) indicate that 46% of surveyed schools, colleges, and departments of education (SCDEs) have partner schools or professional development schools with which they work on a sustained basis (AACTE, 1995). Most PDSs came into existence since 1991 (Abdal-Haqq, 1995b). They are found in urban, suburban, and rural settings in at least 38 states and several foreign countries (Ariav & Clinard, 1996; Duquette & Cook, 1994; Gardner & Libde, 1995; King & Mizoue, 1993; Papoulia-Tzelepi, 1993).

Although the bulk of PDSs are elementary schools (Abdal-Haqq, 1995b), there are also high school, middle school, and junior high school settings. A majority of these sites are public schools, but there are parochial and private schools among them (Fishbaugh & Rose, 1997). PDSs are being planned or implemented in specialized schools for children with emotional disorders (*Professional Development School Programs*, n.d.) and hearing impairments (Martin, 1996) and in juvenile correctional facilities (Radner, Griego, & Wiener, 1994).

A number of states have provided financial resources to support development and implementation of professional development schools, often as part of broader education initiatives: Texas (Warner, 1996); Maryland (Maryland Higher Education Commission, 1995); Massachusetts (Teitel, 1993); South Carolina (Gottesman, Graham, & Nogy, 1993). Minnesota passed legislation to incorporate a mandatory 1-year residency in a PDS into its restructured teacher licensure program (Minnesota State Board of Teaching, 1994). Foundation supporters include AT&T (Abdal-Haqq, in press), Exxon (Levine, 1988), Ford (Anderson, 1993), and Benedum (Hoffman, Reed, & Rosenbluth, 1997) foundations.

Rationale

Critics of American public schools often claim that the structure, agenda, and practices of the prevailing model of schooling inhibit knowledge-based teaching practice and fail to maximize student learning, well-being, or potential. Although this situation shortchanges all students to a greater or lesser degree, historically disadvantaged groups are particularly vulnerable to the consequences of ineffectual schools. According to Ayers (1994):

> All education is about power—its goal is for people to become more skilled, more able, more dynamic, more vital. Teaching is about strengthening, invigorating, and empowering others. Few agree on how to get there, but there is general accord that good teaching enables and strengthens learners. While education is about empowering people, the machinery of schooling is on another mission altogether. Schooling is most often about obedience and conformity; it is about crowd control,

competition, hierarchy and your place in it. It is rule-bound and procedure-driven. Schooling is enervating, and it fosters dependence, passivity, and dullness. In fact, many normal discerning students, wondering what kind of intelligence will be rewarded in school, conclude that being quiet, dull, and invisible is the dominant expectation and act accordingly. Or they drop out altogether. (pp. 224-225)

There is general consensus among education reformers that school restructuring is necessary if schools are to become more enabling and empowering. Effective teachers are seen as central to effective schools. Darling-Hammond states that "a caring and competent teacher for every child in America [is] the critical element needed to reach the goals of education reform" ("A Conversation," 1997, p. 1).

Because existing schools provide the settings for field experiences and student teaching, the prevailing school culture not only fails to promote student learning, it also fails to nourish development of expertise that preservice and novice teachers need to provide enabling and empowering learning experiences for children (Abdal-Haqq, 1991). In essence, today's schools cannot adequately prepare tomorrow's teachers.

Schools designated as PDSs are generally engaged in restructuring. This process may involve changes in organizational and governance structures; redesign of teacher work; reallocation of resources; improvements in the processes of teaching and learning; and changes in the relationships between and among teachers, administrators, school districts, pupils, parents, and higher education institutions (Abdal-Haqq, 1991). Although every PDS setting is distinctive, and restructuring efforts should be context based, the objective of this process in PDSs is to develop models or prototypes of exemplary schools that support positive social and academic development for pupils and improved practice for teachers (Kennedy, 1990, cited in Abdal-Haqq, 1991; Levine, 1988). PDSs are places to determine what works so that findings can be disseminated to other schools. As such, these schools are intended to play a pivotal role in restructuring public schooling.

As models of developing best practice, PDSs also become the most effective settings for clinical training of future teachers. There is considerable evidence that teachers consider their practice teaching experiences to be the most useful element of their professional preparation (Goodlad, 1990; Levine, 1988). There is also considerable evidence that the generally unstructured and idiosyncratic nature of traditional practicums perpetuate many negative teaching practices (Levine, 1988). PDSs are envisioned as sites where structured induction of preservice teachers, as well as continuing development of experienced teachers, is a priority.

Therefore, PDSs play a pivotal role in redesigning and improving preservice and inservice teacher education (Darling-Hammond, 1994). Thus, the PDS becomes the institutional setting where the road to better teacher education and the road to better teaching practice intersect for the benefit of children (National Commission on Teaching, 1996).

Definitions

From the earliest days of the movement, various labels have been applied to schools embodying PDS concepts. In *Tomorrow's Teachers*, the Holmes Group (1986) introduced the term *professional development schools*. The Carnegie report *A Nation Prepared: Teachers for the 21st Century* (1986) called for clinical schools that would serve as practicum settings for rigorous internships for teachers-in-training. The American Federation of Teachers (AFT) piloted professional practice schools in the early years of the movement (Levine, 1992). Lange (1993) provides a useful discussion of the similarities and differences among these three conceptualizations, differences that are essentially a function of the primary agenda of the originators. Other labels include partner school, professional development center, and centers for teaching and learning (Osguthorpe, Harris, Harris, & Black, 1995); professional development academies, induction schools, and teaching schools (Abdal-Haqq, 1991); and centers for professional development and technology (Warner, 1996).

Professional development school is the most widely used label. A Clinical Schools Clearinghouse national survey of 66 partnerships and 300 schools revealed that almost 70% of the respondents refer to their school sites as PDSs, followed by partner school (14%), clinical school (13%), and professional practice school (2%) (Abdal-Haqq, 1995b). Although the names may differ, PDSs share a common set of goals and principles:

- Preparation of preservice teachers and other school-based educators
- Professional development of practicing teachers and other school-based educators
- Exemplary practice designed to maximize student achievement
- Sustained, applied inquiry designed to improve student and educator development

Collaboration is a hallmark of professional development schools. They are partnerships that generally include one or more school districts, one or more colleges or universities, and, in some cases, one or more teachers' unions (Anderson, 1993). PDSs are context oriented and should reflect the geographic, ethnic, and economic diversity of the nation's student population (Holmes Group, 1990; Pasch & Pugach, 1990). PDSs are committed to the simultaneous renewal of both schools and teacher education (Goodlad, 1990). The multiple mission of the PDS is not intended to be assumed by all schools; thus, the number of PDSs should be relatively small when compared to the total number of public schools (Holmes Group, 1990). However, these sites should seek to develop, test, and refine promising practices and structural arrangements that can be utilized by the other schools; therefore, dissemination is a major responsibility of the PDS (Holmes Group, 1990).

Although professional development schools are new institutions in certain respects, they do have antecedents. Elements of the PDS mission are reflected in the university laboratory or campus schools established under the influence of John Dewey. Lange (1993) suggests two reasons for the decline in the number of laboratory schools. They lost their student teaching function to public schools because their somewhat cloistered atmosphere could not emulate public school classrooms; furthermore, the promise of their stated research function remained largely unfulfilled because it had not been given adequate priority or visibility. Portal schools, which operated during the 1960s and 1970s, were public school sites that were intended to develop, test, and disseminate new curriculum and provide authentic settings for initial and inservice teacher education (Lange, 1993; Stallings & Kowalski, 1990). These schools were short-lived, and Stallings and Kowalski speculate that the demise of portal schools may have been due to insufficient evaluation and systematic assessment that could document program effectiveness.

The 600 or so professional development schools that are currently operating are at various stages of development. PDS proponents stress that these institutions are works-in-progress, and full implementation of programming that addresses each of the four major goals is a long-term endeavor. Murray (1993) stresses the developmental character of PDS goals and emphasizes the importance of attending to the total PDS mission: "The goals are interconnected and . . . none can be achieved without the others" (p. 70). An early study of 21 partner or professional development school settings by Brainard (cited in Abdal-Haqq, 1996a) revealed that none of the sites he investigated met all or even most of the 14 indicators he associated with the PDS model. Almost 10 years later, it is evident that rhetoric continues to outstrip reality in many places (Fullan, 1995). Results of this review of the PDS literature suggest that, overall, there has been more movement toward achieving goals associated with preservice and inservice teacher development than toward the other two goals: maximizing student achievement and practice-oriented inquiry.

PDS Literature

As the number of PDSs has grown, so has the volume of literature about them. An ERIC search, using December 1996 CD-ROM editions of the database that are updated about every 3 months, reveals 270 PDS-related abstracts of journal articles and documents. This contrasts sharply with the results of a comparable ERIC search 5 years ago, when fewer than 40 sources—most of which were concept papers of one sort or another—were identified (Abdal-Haqq, 1996a). "Fugitive literature"—newsletters and unpublished project descriptions, reports, proposals, and evaluations—along with electronic resources, audiovisual material, and works-in-progress increases the literature pool.

Three recent reviews have examined PDS literature. In scope, Teitel's (1996) review is the most comprehensive of the three. It provides a panoramic view of the literature and outlines what it reveals about concepts, challenges, and accomplishments. Book (1996) and Valli, Cooper, and Frankes (1997) reviewed PDS research literature. The latter review seeks to match the goals stated by PDS proponents against research-documented changes and links these changes to the PDS equity agenda. The present investigation of PDS literature differs from the aforementioned reviews in three significant ways. First, it incorporates more recent material; second, it includes in the data pool electronic sources, audiovisual material, and sources from fugitive literature; and finally, it may be considered consumer driven.

There is an exciting and informative growth in PDS literature, particularly with regard to issues that threaten to stall or, in some cases, derail efforts to sustain these fledgling institutions. For example, we are seeing more research on various aspects of PDS development and implementation. An ERIC search reveals that research and evaluative reports increased from 11% of ERIC sources in 1991 (Abdal-Haqq, 1996a) to 26% at the end of 1996. The bulk of these studies tend to focus on changes in inservice and preservice teacher attitudes, beliefs, and self-efficacy; examination of development and implementation processes; and investigations of school climate and culture. Case studies have proliferated, often collected in volumes that focus on particular networks such as the National Network for Educational Renewal (Osguthorpe et al., 1995) or the Benedum Collaborative (Hoffman, Reed, & Rosenbluth,

1997), or they appear in more inclusive volumes (Darling-Hammond, 1994; Fishbaugh & Rose, 1997; Petrie, 1995).

There remains a paucity of evaluation studies that document outcomes, particularly student outcomes (Saab, Steel, & Shive, 1997; Valli, Cooper, & Frankes, 1997); however, we are beginning to see some movement in this direction. Overall, more recent PDS literature provides a clearer picture of the processes and activities associated with planning and implementation and is beginning to tell us something about outcomes. In addition, the literature is starting to shed some light on how partnerships may be able to manage some of the thornier issues associated with implementation, such as finding time to do the work and determining costs.

Fugitive literature, audiovisual material, and electronic sources are incorporated into this review for two reasons. First, in many cases, these sources are more current than mainstream literature. Second, this material often provides information that frequently does not appear in more conventional sources (Book, 1996). For example, videos of classroom work in PDS settings can illuminate the kinds of learning experiences PDS practitioners are designing—"glimpses of practice" (Century Communications, 1996; NCREST, 1995; NCREST, 1996). They may help to answer the questions, "What is different about what goes on in a PDS classroom?" and "What distinguishes student teaching in a PDS from what goes on in traditional settings?"

Fugitive literature includes internal or limited-circulation documents, such as proposals or project reports to funding agencies, newsletters, or promotional material. In addition, papers given at regional or state conferences often do not find their way into the education literature mainstream. Nevertheless, these materials can be a rich source of information about programming and even outcomes. For example, an examination of the mainstream literature reveals relatively little information about the types of inquiry going on in PDSs. However, a scan of program newsletters, which generally have heavy input from school-based faculty, reveals that collaborative and individual research is occurring and that results from these inquiries are being used to enhance student learning. Information that appears in fugitive sources may eventually find its way into conference papers or journal articles, but the lag time can be considerable, and, in some cases, this information does not seem to find its way into open-air channels at all. Researchers who slight fugitive literature because it may not be accessed as easily as more conventional sources have a legitimate complaint. For this reason, when such material is cited in this review, I have included information on the reference list that should facilitate locating the source.

The Internet and World Wide Web are becoming increasingly useful sources of information about professional development schools. At present, electronic sources are not numerous, and their informational value varies. They range from Web sites that have one-page statements that say no more than "Hi! We're a new PDS partnership" to Gopher and Web sites that post transcripts of interviews with prominent PDS educators (Michigan State University, 1995) or in-depth case studies (Swanson, 1995). Electronic sources are attractive dissemination venues for underfunded programs because they can be cost-effective and because they reduce the time lag between producing a document and disseminating it. For example, I located on the Michigan State University Web site a very informative report that reviewed the history and accomplishments of the university's PDS network several months before the report came across my desk in print form (Judge, Carriedo, & Johnson, 1995).

This review is very much shaped by queries that I have received while coordinating the Clinical Schools Clearinghouse (CSC). The clearinghouse collects, generates, processes, and disseminates information about professional development schools. It is also a part of the ERIC system and functions as the Adjunct ERIC Clearinghouse on Clinical Schools. ERIC is the major dissemination vehicle employed by the clearinghouse for the PDS literature that it collects, and the bulk of the sources to be found in the ERIC database at present were abstracted by clearinghouse staff. During the last 6 years, I have fielded hundreds of questions from teachers, professors, school district and building administrators, researchers, students, legislators, and journalists. The persistence and consistency of recurring themes among the inquiries suggest to me that there are certain core concerns that preoccupy practitioners, observers, and decision makers. I have been guided in my exploration of the PDS literature by these concerns. This review attempts to extract from the literature an illuminating profile of what actually goes on in PDS settings, convey what is known about the benefits of PDS programming for certain stakeholders, provide some insight into how partnerships are meeting some of the common challenges to program implementation, and highlight issues and areas where the literature is ominously silent.

Methodology

The six guiding questions listed below were used as navigational aids for this exploration of the professional development school literature.

1. What are the characteristics of initial teacher preparation, professional development, teaching and learning, and inquiry in PDS settings?
2. What outcomes are reported, and how are they determined?
3. How are PDS partnerships meeting two common challenges to program implementation—time and financing?
4. Is PDS programming commonly merged with other reform initiatives or innovations—specifically, integrated services programs, technology infusion, and parent involvement?
5. Are there characteristics typically associated with initial teacher preparation in PDSs that may restrict access for low-income students or students from ethnic or language minority groups, and how have PDS partnerships addressed this issue?
6. Does PDS programming explicitly address the needs of historically marginalized or vulnerable learners?

After formulating the six guiding questions, I scanned the ERIC sources, as well as the fugitive literature and works-in-progress I was able to acquire, for material relevant to each question. A major selection criterion was timeliness; for the most part, I have focused on literature produced between 1992 and 1997. Other factors include the maturity of the partnership in question when program descriptions are considered and the focus and methodology employed in research reports. More mature partnerships have generally gained through trial and error a rich storehouse of knowledge about developmental processes and how to overcome common obstacles. In addition, they are often at a point where they can begin to meaningfully assess effectiveness and outcomes.

Book (1996) and others point out that descriptive studies predominate in the PDS literature, but often, insufficient description of research methodology leaves readers with questions about the validity or replicability of these studies. The reviews by Book and by Valli, Cooper, and Frankes (1997) provide informative critiques of the methodologies employed in the studies they reviewed. Few evaluative, quantitative, or empirical studies have surfaced in the literature, particularly studies that focus on the impact of PDS programming on students in schools. Most studies focus on

1. Attitudes, self-efficacy, satisfaction, and beliefs of teachers, university faculty, and student teachers
2. Collaborative processes and developmental issues
3. New roles for P-12 and university faculty
4. Inquiry that takes place within PDS settings (Berry, Boles, Edens, Nissenholtz, & Trachtman, 1996; Book, 1996; Scannell, 1996; Teitel, 1996)

Thus, for the most part, the research highlighted in this review focuses on topics that heretofore have not been widely investigated; is characterized by quantitative, empirical, or multiple methodologies; or has been reported within the last 2 years. This book is not intended to be an exhaustive review of the current body of PDS literature. It is deliberately selective, focusing on what the literature tells us about certain key concerns and, it is hoped, highlighting critical issues to which the PDS literature has thus far given limited attention.

1

Teacher Development in Professional Development School Settings

This chapter examines the features and practices that characterize initial teacher preparation and professional development for practicing teachers in PDSs. In addition, the impact of teacher development programming on participants, as reported in the PDS literature, will be considered. The chapter highlights recent related research and concludes with a brief discussion of gaps in the literature that suggest areas in need of further exploration.

Preservice Preparation

Program Features and Practices

Overall, the literature is relatively expansive about both the features and the effects of initial teacher preparation in PDS settings. When compared to traditional preservice teacher education, initial teacher preparation in PDSs

1. Incorporates earlier, longer, and more structured clinical experiences (Fountain & Evans, 1994; Hecht, Bland, Schoon, & Boschert, 1996; Trachtman, 1996)
2. Involves school-based faculty to a greater degree in the design and implementation of coursework and field experiences (Trachtman, 1996)
3. Is more likely to be a postbaccalaureate program (Lyons, 1996)

4. Provides more frequent and sustained supervision and feedback (Fountain & Evans, 1994; Hayes & Wetherill, 1996)

5. Employs more varied assessment strategies, including portfolios and other performance assessment mechanisms (Houston et al., 1995; Lyons, 1996)

6. Exposes students to more diverse, authentic learning experiences (Rasch & Finch, 1996)

7. Strives to be more supportive, reflective, and empowering (Lieberman & Miller, 1992)

In addition, coursework is more likely to be site based, collaboratively developed and taught by school-college faculty teams, and linked to both the professional development of inservice teachers and school needs and priorities (Hayes & Wetherill, 1996; Newman et al., 1996; Wiseman & Cooner, 1996).

It is common for student teachers in PDSs to be involved in schoolwide restructuring or curriculum initiatives (Crawford, Smith, Thacker, Turner, & Watkins, 1993; Jett-Simpson, Pugach, & Whipp, 1992). They generally are more immersed in the day-to-day life of the schools to which they are assigned, their fieldwork involves them in noninstructional activities, and they routinely interact with members of the school community besides their assigned cooperating teacher (Barba, Seideman, Schneider, & Mera, 1993; Wiseman & Cooner, 1996). They are more likely than their peers in traditional programs to add value to the school program, supplementing the work of regular staff with students through activities like after-school tutoring, taking charge of specific projects such as developing handbooks or supervising an extracurricular activity for children, or substituting for teachers when time is needed for professional development or committee work (Houston et al., 1995; Lemlech, Hertzog-Foliart, & Hackl, 1994). Student teachers are typically placed in clusters or cohorts, and they may be assigned to a classroom in teams (Hausfather, Outlaw, & Strehle, 1996). They usually have a mentor who may or may not be the same individual who functions as the cooperating teacher (Barba et al., 1993). Selection criteria and procedures for both interns and cooperating teachers tend to be more rigorous in PDS preservices programs than in more traditional programs (Hayes & Wetherill, 1996).

Preservice Outcomes

The literature conveys the general impression that preservice teachers whose practicum experiences take place in PDS settings, in contrast to traditional student teaching placements,

1. Utilize more varied pedagogical methods and practices (Miller & O'Shea, 1994; Zeichner, 1992)
2. Are more reflective (Hayes & Wetherill, 1996)
3. Enter teaching with more knowledge of school routine and activities beyond the classroom (Trachtman, 1996)
4. Feel more confidence in their knowledge and skill as professionals and subsequently experience less "culture shock" when they become practicing teachers (Book, 1996; Tusin, 1995)
5. Feel themselves to be better equipped to instruct ethnically and linguistically diverse student populations and are more likely to seek employment in inner-city schools when their practicums stress work in urban areas (Abdal-Haqq, in press; Arends & Winitzky, 1996)
6. Have lower attrition rates during the first few years of teaching and are more likely to "hit the ground running" when they become employed (Hayes & Wetherill, 1996; *The Model Clinical Teaching Program*, n.d.)

The evidence substantiating these impressions is largely found in graduate follow-up studies; surveys of attitudes, beliefs, and self-efficacy; collections of student interviews or reviews of student journals; and other self-reporting mechanisms (Abdal-Haqq, 1996a; Berry et al. 1996; Teitel, 1996). Project descriptions and case studies frequently include personal narratives and other anecdotal evidence attesting to the positive effects of the PDS on preservice teachers. Although the nontraditional preservice practices and programming commonly found in PDSs seem to produce productive and satisfying field experiences for interns, the literature does supply examples of cases in which interns experience higher levels of stress than their peers (Hopkins, Hoffman, & Moss, 1997).

Some evidence is available that preservice teachers who do their fieldwork in PDSs outperform, on some measures, their peers in traditional programs. For example, Houston et al. (1995) report that elementary certification candidates in their PDS-based program scored 15 to 34 percentage points higher than their peers in the traditional program on each of the basic tests of Texas's required examination for teacher licensure. The authors also report that PDS graduates of programs in the Houston Consortium for Professional Development and Technology Centers are greatly sought after by schools seeking new teachers. School principals in the AT&T Teachers for Tomorrow program also emphasize the desirability of new teachers who have gone through intense clinical experiences in PDS settings (Abdal-Haqq, in press). Miller and O'Shea (1994) report that program graduates of the Southern Maine Partnership are hired in record numbers. The literature also includes references to the regard in which PDS-based programs are held by state accrediting bodies (Ariav & Clinard, 1996).

Few longitudinal studies of PDS graduates seem to have been done, so it is unclear if significant numbers of graduates remain in teaching; seek and continue employment in inner-city or isolated rural schools, which typically find it hard to attract and retain well-qualified teachers; or routinely employ innovative, research-based practices that they encounter in PDS preparation. The scarcity of information on these issues is due in part to the newness of PDSs and partly to the failure on the part of most partnerships to adequately follow up and document their graduates' progress. Both the mainstream and the fugitive literature contain isolated statistics and anecdotal evidence indicating that program graduates remain in teaching and seek employment in inner-city schools. For example, a pamphlet that describes the Model Clinical Teaching Program (MCTP), a partnership between East Carolina University and Pitt County (NC) public schools, indicates that results of a 5-year study of program graduates show that almost 98% of MCTP graduates have remained in the classroom, compared to a national average of less than 60% (*The Model Clinical Teaching Program*, n.d.).

Recent Research

THE PROFESSIONAL DEVELOPMENT SCHOOL STANDARDS PROJECT

Trachtman (1996) conducted a survey of 28 "highly developed" professional development school sites for the Professional Development School Standards Project as part of the project's effort to develop a consensus about mission and good practice in PDSs. The data collection instrument, an "open-ended questionnaire which would allow participants to 'talk' to us by talking with each other" (p. 5), addressed goals the participants had set, how they were working to meet the goals, their view of supporting and constraining conditions, and how they measured progress in attaining their goals.

Sixty-five percent of the respondents indicated that preservice teachers spend more time in the field in the PDS-based program than in their traditional programs. Preservice teachers are usually assigned to a site in cohorts and are sometimes assigned in pairs to a classroom. Eighty-five percent of the respondents indicated that preservice teachers work with school-based teams that have various functions, such as curriculum development, action research, and creating performance assessments. Trachtman's data suggest that PDS preservice teachers become a buildingwide responsibility and in turn are more immersed in the daily life of the school. These preservice teachers add value to the classroom and the school by providing additional services to students and permitting inservice teachers to engage in alternative professional work.

Preservice teachers are engaged in research about practice at more than 75% of the sites. More than 90% of the respondents indicate that at least one preservice course is located at the school site. This coursework may be facilitated by either university or school faculty. In more than 50% of the sites, school-based teachers hold college appointments; they collaboratively plan teacher education curriculum in more than 80% of the sites; and in 60% of the partnerships surveyed, they participate in activities associated with university renewal. University faculty are teaching children at more than half of the sites; most respondents report university faculty participation in school-based councils and committees that focus on school renewal; and 89% indicate that university and school faculty work together to plan professional development activities.

Anecdotal evidence provided some sense of survey participants' perceptions of program outcomes, but Trachtman indicates that systematic follow-up of graduates was not evident among respondents. Sites reported that graduates appear to begin their professional careers with greater knowledge and more skills than their peers; they have greater understanding of diversity and the nonacademic needs of students; they are more committed and self-confident and are more likely to reach out to others and participate in schoolwide activities.

THE TEACHERS COLLEGE OF EMPORIA STATE UNIVERSITY

Long (1996) reports results from two studies of PDS interns at The Teachers College of Emporia State University. Sixteen elementary education majors spent a one-year internship working in elementary classrooms under the supervision of mentor teachers, university faculty, and a full-time on-site coordinator in a program described as 100% field based and collaborative. To assess first-year results, the 16 PDS interns were compared to a control group of 16 students who were completing the campus-based teacher preparation program during the same period. Methods of evaluation included portfolios, research questionnaires, the Attitude Towards Mainstreaming Scale, and the National Teacher Examination (NTE) Professional Knowledge Test.

The Teacher Education Questionnaire was used as a pre- and post-test measure, and a t test produced significant differences between the two groups on only 25 of the 309 items found on the questionnaire. No significant post differences were found between the NTE scores of the PDS interns and the control group. However, results from the Attitude Towards Mainstreaming Scale did indicate that the PDS group was significantly more positive toward inclusion than the control group. Researchers concluded that, overall, the program was successful and that first-year graduates compared very favorably with their peers in the campus-based program.

Long's study of 20 second-year interns focused on goal accomplishment and did not incorporate a matched pair design. Indirect assessment involved examination of materials (portfolios, lesson plans, and logs) submitted by PDS interns. Direct assessment of 12 instructional and professional outcomes was based on four measures.

Results of the indirect assessment generally corresponded to self-reported perceptions, indicating a favorable degree of internalization of program goals. The mentor teacher survey revealed that the interns showed definite improvement in goal attainment activities as the semester progressed. Results of the student teaching questionnaire, administered to PDS and non-PDS students, show that PDS interns perceived themselves as more effectively prepared for classroom teaching in all facets of the program. Results of the post teacher confidence survey indicated that PDS interns did not differ significantly from their peers in subject matter preparation and that PDS interns felt significantly more secure on nine indicators of pedagogical effectiveness. Although a range of performance levels emerged from the classroom management assessment, PDS interns generally demonstrated a favorable level of competence and employed classroom management techniques endorsed by both experienced classroom teachers and university faculty.

Long concluded that evidence from the first 2 years of PDS programming indicates that the PDS program produces a "highly competent student, well versed in pedagogical theory" (p. 13). PDS interns appear to develop during the student-teaching semester at a rate somewhat faster than their peers. Future research will include following graduates of both programs for a year and assessing the degree to which observed differences persist into regular teaching performance.

UNIVERSITY OF NORTH CAROLINA—WILMINGTON

Hayes and Wetherill (1996) report results of a comprehensive evaluation of a PDS partnership between the University of North Carolina—Wilmington and two school districts. The evaluation, completed in 1994-1995, employed a variety of formative and summative assessment mechanisms to examine program impact on schools, teachers, preservice teachers, and teacher education programs. A 1995 follow-up study of program graduates collected data on the status and performance of PDS graduates as beginning teachers.

Findings related to preservice preparation indicate that public school personnel consider program graduates to be better prepared for the role of teacher and teacher leader. Interns perceived themselves to be more capable as a result of the program than they would have been in other programs. The school of education has adopted key elements of the model for implementation with the entire student-teaching program. The process of intern, university, and clinical teacher supervision has changed to incorporate

1. Skill development by supervisors
2. A developmental approach to supervision
3. A more reflective and critical examination of teaching focus
4. More individualized supervisory strategies

The follow-up study utilized data from telephone interviews with principals who had employed program graduates. Principals were asked to compare, in six areas, program graduates with other teachers at the same experience level. Forty-one of the 58 clinical interns who graduated from the program between fall 1993 and spring 1995 were employed as public school teachers. Although all of the school administrators indicated that program graduates were well prepared for teaching, 80% felt they were much better prepared. Strong performance areas included classroom management, knowledge and use of varied classroom strategies, and planning. Program graduates were more likely to "hit the ground running" than their peers. Administrators indicated that graduates were distinguished by their ability to engage in self-analysis, to problem solve, and to capitalize on available resources. With regard to overall impact on their schools, the administrators considered program graduates to be positive role models for risk taking and employing innovative strategies; they contributed to a positive collaborative school climate and to the schools' renewal efforts.

Professional Development

The literature offers a fairly revealing portrait of professional development activities for inservice teachers in PDS settings. These activities take many forms, and collectively their objective extends beyond the conventional purpose of staff development. The customary approach to inservice teacher education has, for the most part, reflected a deficit model of teacher learning. In many ways, this model reflects the traditional approach to teaching and learning for students—clients (i.e., teachers or students) are fed discrete doses of information by an "expert." The client rarely has a say in what he or she needs to know and has even less to say about how information is delivered. Typically, such decisions are made by individuals and entities that are removed from the schools and communities where clients perform their work and live their lives.

Program Features and Practices

Professional development in PDSs differs from traditional professional development in several ways. First, teachers themselves participate to a larger degree in the design, focus, and implementation of professional development activities. Activities are more closely linked to local needs and priorities, which are more likely to be identified by school personnel (Wiseman & Cooner, 1996), as well as district or state directives (Houston et al., 1995). Their focus is generally broader than enhancement of individual skills (Crow, Stokes, Kauchak, Hobbs, & Bullough, Jr., 1996); professional development in PDSs is intended to increase the capacity of teachers to actively participate in the change processes associated with school and teacher education renewal. Ideally, professional development in PDS settings is enabling and empowering; a major objective is to engage teachers in the effort to move teaching closer to being a profession that sets its own standards of practice and is accountable to students, parents, and communities (Darling-Hammond, 1994; Holmes Group, 1986).

Professional development in PDS settings includes traditional formats such as formal coursework, summer institutes, and retreats (Hausfather, Outlaw, & Strehle, 1996; Houston et al., 1995; Newman et al., 1996). It may also include site-based study groups that focus on curriculum topics such as classroom management, cooperative learning, or literacy instruction (Trachtman, 1996). These study groups often include preservice teachers and college faculty (Devlin-Scherer, 1993). Teachers in PDSs frequently engage in more active learning venues, such as action research and other forms of systematic inquiry; site-based management teams; instruction, mentoring, and supervision of preservice interns (Collinson, Hohenbrink, Sherrill, & Bible, 1994; Crow et al., 1996); and professional development for other teachers (Fountain & Evans, 1994). Professional development in PDSs encourages reflection and self-analysis (Anderson et al., 1995; Devlin-Scherer, 1993); it seeks to establish a norm of continuous learning; and it offers opportunities for teachers to perfect continuous learning strategies. Formal and informal support mechanisms are common characteristics (Bullough, Jr., Kauchack, Crow, Hobbs, & Stokes, 1997b). It places teachers at the center of school change and renewal and aims to produce teachers who are not only skilled practitioners but who also have the capacity to function as change agents (Crow et al., 1996).

Teachers in PDSs take on nontraditional roles. Both school and university faculty engaged in PDS work are frequently called "bicultural" or "boundary spanners" in the literature because they cross conventional lines of demarcation between school and university cultures and/or between roles within a particular culture (Teitel, 1997b). For example, the duties of teacher facilitators in the PDS partnership between University of Utah and two local school districts include intern mentoring, quasi-administrative responsibilities for facilitating PDS growth and development, and occasional teacher inservice (Bullough, Jr. et al., 1997b). In the Southern Maine Partnership, school faculty who work as site coordinators and mentors have adjunct status at the university (Lyons, 1996). School-based teacher instructors form collaborative instructional teams with faculty from Indiana University—Northwest and design an urban-focused curriculum for preservice students placed in Gary, Indiana PDSs (Sandoval, Reed, & Attinasi, 1993).

Fountain and Evans (1994) describe a number of redesigned school and university faculty roles. Preinternship Excelling in Clinical Education Learning (EXCEL) clinical educators are exemplary classroom teachers who hold 2-year joint assignments with the University of North Florida and local school districts. Their time is divided between conducting preinternship field-based seminars for teacher education students and working with collaborative school-based teams that address district concerns. Resident clinical faculty (RCFs) are exemplary classroom teachers who also hold 2-year joint university-school district appointments. Two are assigned to each PDS and have a number of responsibilities: planning and supervising the internship experience in cooperation with classroom directing (cooperating) teachers and university personnel, assisting colleagues in implementing school improvement plans, and planning and conducting on-site inquiry seminars for interns. Along with university faculty, RCFs attend biweekly inquiry seminars on the university campus. The seminars focus on school improvement initiatives, adult learning, clinical supervision, supporting the professional growth of novice teachers, and the change process.

Professional Development Outcomes

Some of the earliest attempts to document the impact of PDS programming focused on teacher outcomes. For the most part the research focused on self-reported changes in beliefs, self-efficacy, and satisfaction. In these studies, attitude surveys, interviews, reviews of reflective journals, personal narratives, and anecdotes were commonly used to collect data and document teacher outcomes (Book, 1996). Often these outcomes become evident as a result of school climate surveys (Abdal-Haqq, 1996a). The preponderance of research on teachers in PDSs continues to reflect these formats; however, more recent research includes a number of case studies that attempt to document change processes and enhancers and obstacles to teacher development (Bell, 1995; Swanson, 1995; Whitford, 1994).

Overall, the literature indicates that significant numbers of practicing teachers benefit from their involvement in PDS programming. Teachers report

1. More willingness to take instructional risks and experiment with new content and approaches (Houston Consortium, 1996)
2. Being intellectually stimulated and energized by exposure to new ideas; opportunities to conduct school-based research; and collegial interaction with peers, preservice teachers, and university faculty (Trachtman, 1996)
3. Growth from engaging in nontraditional roles (Collinson et al., 1994; Wiseman & Cooner, 1996)
4. Less isolation (Ariav & Clinard, 1996; Barba et al., 1993)
5. Less powerlessness (Crow et al., 1996; Neufeld & McGowan, 1993)
6. Improvements in their classroom practice (Crow et al., 1996; Houston Consortium, 1996)
7. A greater feeling of professionalism (Morris & Nunnery, 1993)

Teachers find their PDS work enabling and empowering; greater teacher satisfaction and improved morale are frequently reported in the literature (Jett-Simpson, Pugach, & Whipp, 1992).

Trachtman's (1996) survey of 28 PDS partnerships documented a number of outcomes for inservice teachers, including changes in classroom practice, confidence in their own knowledge, stimulation by PDS involvement and public recognition, and determining their own professional development needs. "In the PDS it appears as though teachers' growth comes from and through teachers' practice; learning takes place in the context of thinking and acting as a teacher" (p. 24).

Much of the PDS literature on outcomes for teachers focuses on teacher leadership and the challenges of assuming new, noninstructional roles. Teitel (1997b) indicates that

the inter-organizational aspects of PDS partnerships means teachers need to serve as liaisons and boundary spanners working to bridge gaps between the world of schools and colleges . . . leadership in PDSs is more broadly inclusive and presumed for many teachers. At work is nothing less than a redefinition of what a professional teacher does—one that calls for a substantial role outside of the classroom. (p. 13)

Assuming new roles and expanding the range of activities in which they engage frequently creates personal and professional stress and pressures for teachers (Abdal-Haqq, 1996b). Conflicts with colleagues, administrators, and university faculty over "turf" issues can emerge. Teitel (1997b) also points out that gender issues can constitute an undercurrent of tension when members of the largely female teaching force move out of their accustomed "place" in the decision-making hierarchy. Extra demands on teachers' time are an additional source of strain (Troen & Bolles, 1994). In addition, dedicated teachers often experience guilt over "deserting" their classrooms to engage in planning, professional development, supervision, or collaborative activities (Abdal-Haqq, 1996b; Collinson et al., 1994). Trachtman (1996, p. 26) also identifies "systemic constraints" to teacher learning, including local school board limits on the amount of time teachers can spend away from their classrooms and traditional approaches to teacher evaluation that do not recognize or reward new knowledge and skills. Isolation from colleagues and invisibility within the university are also reported by teachers who step out of their traditional roles (Chase, Merryfield, & Chism, 1996; Collinson et al., 1994). In discussing the difficulties of being a boundary spanner, Bullough, Jr. et al. (1997a) refer to the "clinical ghetto" (p. 91) to which teachers who become clinical faculty are sometimes consigned.

Professional development schools vary in their attention to the training and support teachers may need to function effectively in these new roles. The most common accommodation is providing coursework or seminars on supervision or mentoring (Ariav & Clinard, 1996), although it is not uncommon for teachers to assume these responsibilities with little or no training or orientation (Newman et al., 1996). In addition, without an adequate communication infrastructure within the partnership, these teacher leaders may find themselves adrift and floundering (Hecht et al., 1996).

Until recently, there have been very few examples in the literature of systematic attempts to correlate reported teacher growth with changes in classroom practice, student performance, or schoolwide change. For the most part, we had some anecdotal and inferential evidence that PDS professional development programming resulted in changes in practice, expanded repertoires of instructional strategies, better classroom and school environments, and positive impact on the achievement and behavior of students. Although evidence that professional development translates into improvements for students and schools is not abundant, the literature does report some examples. In addition, PDS literature is beginning to show that efforts are underway to systematically document teacher change and the impact of that change on schools and students.

Recent Research

UNIVERSITY OF WISCONSIN—MILWAUKEE
/MILWAUKEE PUBLIC SCHOOLS

Jett-Simpson, Pugach, and Whipp (1992) utilized interviews and observation to document individual and collective changes in teachers and the impact of the changes on students that resulted from efforts to implement redesigned literacy instruction in an urban PDS. University and school faculty collaborated on changing the prevailing language arts instructional paradigm, which is described as "a decontextualized, skill-driven approach grounded in the use of basal texts and workbooks . . . [and characterized by] a focus on the children's academic deficits" (p. 3). In the second full year of the partnership, school and college faculty agreed on a set of broad goals for the school's literacy program, and two of these goals—to increase the time children devoted to reading and to develop greater interest in and positive attitudes about reading— became the main focus of professional development for the 1990-1991 school year.

The new instructional paradigm focused on developing an integrated language-arts program that embedded instruction in reading authentic materials, such as children's literature, and performing authentic writing tasks. Periodic staff meetings and half-day sessions on contemporary approaches to literacy instruction were held; university liaisons worked directly with individual teachers, provided classroom demonstrations, and engaged in co-teaching. The majority of teachers developed and implemented action research projects that focused on an aspect of their literacy instruction they wanted to change. Preservice teachers were placed at the PDS site where they were able to observe and participate in making the transition to a more child-centered approach.

Data were collected from 34 teachers using a piloted semistructured interview schedule. As a source of triangulation regarding schoolwide change, self-reports by teachers were supplemented with interviews with specialists (e.g., in art, science, music) who regularly move from class to class. Researchers examined three aspects of change that took place since redesigned literacy instruction was implemented: patterns of teacher change, schoolwide change, and student change. Results indicate varied patterns of change in teachers' instructional practices. Teachers reported better teacher and student morale, more enthusiasm and interest in reading and writing on the part of students, and less fighting and other antisocial behavior among students. Teachers also indicated that students seemed to be utilizing their developing literacy skills across the curriculum. The authors concluded that "the professional development school provided a positive, supportive environment for change" (p. 19).

THE LEARNING-TEACHING COLLABORATIVE

Boles and Troen (1994) conducted a study that examined the development of leadership skills and roles among teachers in the Learning-Teaching Collaborative (L-TC). L-TC is characterized by schoolwide team teaching, school-university collaboration, special education inclusion, and alternative professional time (APT). APT allows teachers at least one pupil-free day per week to assume nontraditional roles or engage in alternative professional work (e.g., curriculum writer, researcher, student teacher supervisor, college teacher). The combination of team teaching and full-time student teacher interns enables this schedule to work. Eight L-TC teachers were interviewed for this study, and findings indicate that a nontraditional leadership paradigm is emerging at the PDS.

Teacher leadership in the L-TC is characterized by a form of collective leadership that permits teachers to develop expertise reflecting individual interests. The eight teachers who were interviewed for the study indicated that the PDS nurtured teacher leadership, leadership activities grew naturally out of professional interests and working teams, teaching practices changed significantly, and professional relationships improved.

UNIVERSITY OF UTAH—SALT LAKE CITY

Through cross-case analysis, Bullough, Jr. et al. (1997b) explored the impact of involvement in professional development schools on teachers' professional growth and on school change at four elementary and three secondary sites established by the University of Utah—Salt Lake City and two local school districts. Data were collected from questionnaires and interviews with 49 teachers and principals. Between 1990 and 1993, a site-based Cooperative Masters (Co-op) degree program was established at each of the seven PDSs in the partnership. Teachers who are enrolled in the Co-ops meet at the school site and stay together as a group for 2 years with a university instructor who coordinates and teaches in the program. During the second year of the program, teachers typically participate in action research as a means of engaging in systematic study of their own teaching practice. The analysis related key program elements and participants' roles to areas of teacher change, school change and learning environment, and conceptions of teacher education. In addition, data were collected and analyzed on target themes.

Teachers reported changes in classroom practice and increased reflectivity, often linked to working with teacher candidates. Teachers also recounted increased faculty interaction and improved morale. However, reported changes in reflection and teaching practices did not appear to affect teachers' views that theory is of limited value to teacher candidates when compared to the practical experience gained from student teaching. Teachers implicitly advocated the apprenticeship model of teacher education, and among secondary teachers, the theme that "teachers are born, not made" emerged. Most teachers held fairly limited conceptions of the PDS mission. They saw it primarily as a place to train teacher candidates, exposing them to the difference between what the university was telling them and the reality of teaching, and as an opportunity to prepare them to survive the first year of teaching and fit into school culture. Fewer teachers appeared to recognize the PDS as an environment for teacher growth and renewal, and still fewer emphasized collaborative research and inquiry. Lack of involvement, poor communication, lack of building leadership, and ineffective inservice activities appeared to be relevant in cases when teacher change did not occur. Effective mechanisms for teacher change appear to be connected to firsthand intensive and extensive experiences, particularly interaction with teacher candidates; serving as teacher facilitators and serving on site steering committees; and participation in the Co-op program. Inservice activities sponsored by the university were generally dismissed as superficial and irrelevant to teacher needs.

Lacunae

Noticeably missing from PDS literature on teacher development are adequate follow-up studies that track preservice teachers after they enter the profession. Although some data and anecdotal information can be found, it is insufficient to buttress claims that PDSs in general produce teachers who are more employable or proficient. In addition, effective teacher development ideally equips teachers to simultaneously look inward—examining their personal attitudes, practices, expectations—and outward, to the school community beyond their classrooms and the larger community beyond the school grounds. Follow-up studies that document the extent to which teachers involved in PDS preparation programs adhere to the principles of reflection, collegiality, and accountability are needed to assess PDS effectiveness in promoting these attributes. Such studies might not only evaluate impact but also provide guidelines for program modification and for the kinds of ongoing support needed. A final reason for following newly hatched PDS fledglings is the need to determine how they fare in "traditional schools." Although the PDS strives to become tomorrow's school, the bulk of its graduates for the immediate future will find employment in today's schools. Scannell (1996) lists a number of variables that might productively be included in follow-up studies of preservice and inservice teachers in PDSs, as well as studies of impact on students.

Another void in the literature relates to reports of conclusive links between teacher development and student achievement, a linkage that is likely to become a make-or-break issue for PDSs. Although some progress is evident, the overall paucity of convincing data is disturbing.

This chapter has focused on teacher development, but the PDS mission includes attention to the education of other school-based educators as well. The literature suggests that there is relatively little programming going on in this regard. This too constitutes a potentially serious constraint on the overall impact that PDSs can have.

Finally, much of PDS literature is devoted to the collaborative processes that enable programs to develop and grow. We read a lot about the importance of teachers' voices in shaping and directing these collaboratives. What we do not hear are the voices of students, parents, and relevant community stakeholders being raised in the chambers where decisions about program focus, direction, and content are made. Nor do we hear these voices when it is time to determine program effectiveness. Webb-Dempsey's (1997) report on the assessment of PDSs in the Benedum Collaborative provides compelling evidence that student voices can be particularly valuable as gauges of program success. The report confirms that students can be shrewd judges of teaching quality. More accounts from these neglected stakeholders would make a worthy contribution to PDS literature.

2

Student Learning and Inquiry

Of the four primary goals or purposes that shape the mission of professional development schools, inquiry and student achievement have received the least systematic attention in the PDS literature (Berry et al., 1996; Saab, Steel, & Shive, 1997; Teitel, 1996; Valli, Cooper, & Frankes, 1997). Not only is there little conclusive evidence that PDS programs produce sustained improvements in students' academic and social development, the literature also fails to give us more than a sketchy description of P-12 teaching and learning activities.

This situation is disquieting for two reasons. First, if children are not significantly benefiting from the investment of time, effort, and resources devoted to PDSs, then both children and investors are being betrayed. Children are captives of the schools society creates; they are the trust of educators, policymakers, legislators, and funders whose moral obligation as stewards requires that they deploy scarce resources in ways that promote and secure the well-being of children. Thus, human and fiscal resources invested in professional development schools are squandered if PDS implementers do not at least attempt to devise, test, refine, and document effective curriculum and practices.

The second cause for disquiet has both pragmatic and moral dimensions. If, in fact, substantive work aimed at enhancing student learning is being done in PDS settings, positive results of this work can buttress arguments that continued investment in professional development schools is warranted. In addition, if PDS implementers are discovering or confirming productive practices and structures, they have a moral obligation to disseminate their findings where the results can do the most good.

The bulk of mainstream PDS literature focuses on preservice and inservice teacher development and the processes and results of collaboration, with limited attention given to student learning. Common sense and justice demand that one be cautious in reading too much into sheer volume, but the imbalance is suggestive. It suggests that student learning has heretofore been of secondary importance to PDS programmers. As a parent or a taxpayer or a fundamentally decent sort of person, I may take tepid pleasure in knowing that teachers are feeling happier, more professional, and more empowered or that schools and colleges are interacting more amicably, but I still want to know what it all means for my children and other children, now and in the years to come. Lipman (1997) and others (Dempsey, 1997; Meyers, 1996) point out that teacher empowerment and professionalization, as well as other flagships of contemporary restructuring efforts, such as school-based teacher development (Fullan, 1995), are not sufficient by themselves to bring about more equitable and appropriate learning experiences for children. Without reflection and action on the fundamental assumptions, priorities, and values that undergird public school instruction, children, particularly children from marginalized groups, will continue to be shortchanged. Thus far, the PDS literature has not been particularly informative about whether increased school-college collaboration, altered models of teacher development, or reported changes in preservice and inservice teacher attitudes and behaviors translate into improved outcomes for students.

Inquiry in PDS settings and inquiry about outcomes, particularly outcomes related to student achievement, have also received limited attention in the literature. Inquiry is considered by many to be a distinguishing feature of the PDS, a feature that sets it apart from other school reform initiatives, as well as a key component and enabler of the learning community PDS proponents seek to establish in these sites (Ishler & Edens, 1995).

This chapter examines what PDS literature reports about the activities, characteristics, and outcomes of PDS programming that targets student achievement. Inquiry in PDSs and inquiry about PDS effectiveness are also discussed. These two facets of the PDS mission are linked for two reasons. First, inquiry and reflection are intimately connected to the kind of teaching and learning PDS proponents seek to establish. Second, inquiry about PDS effectiveness facilitates accountability and is a key to establishing credibility. The discussion begins with a summary of major themes and concepts that ideally define teaching and learning in PDSs. I then relate examples of programs attempting to implement practices reflecting these concepts and themes and some of the reported findings related to student outcomes.

Several themes related to student learning emerged from this review. First, although information about innovative curriculum and instructional practices, as well as outcomes, is not abundant, it does appear. We frequently find it embedded in studies or program descriptions that have collaboration or teacher development as their primary focus. Second, these scattered glimpses of practice and reports of outcomes are often found in fugitive, audiovisual, and electronic sources. Although such sources may lack the rigor and accessibility that researchers and academics treasure, as supplements to mainstream literature they provide reassuring evidence that student learning is not entirely neglected or taken for granted in PDSs. Third, there is encouraging evidence that PDS implementers are mounting systematic investigations and beginning to collect data on how programming affects students, some results from these investigations are beginning to appear in the mainstream literature, and partnerships are beginning to embed ongoing documentation and evaluation into program design.

Student Learning

Conceptual Framework

In discussions about PDS principles or undergirding concepts, certain phrases recur when teaching practice and student learning are addressed: *teaching for understanding, learner-centered schools, learning communities, child-centered practice, all children can learn,* and *ambitious teaching* (Holmes Group, 1990, 1995; Pechman, 1992; "Vision Statement," 1993).

In addition to providing a scenario of what teaching for understanding might look like in practice, Ishler and Edens (1995) connect this concept to inquiry and reflection, collaboration, and the community of learners.

> Teaching for understanding requires that the teacher become a facilitator and co-constructor of knowledge with students through posing questions, challenging student thinking, and leading them in examining ideas and relationships. In doing so the classroom emerges as a community of learners that supports thoughtful learning, inquiry, connecting ideas, and collaboration. This conceptualization of teaching defines knowledge as being constructed and therefore situated in prior experiences and existing conceptions (and misconceptions) of learners. . . . Students, teachers, administrators, staff, parents, and the community-at-large are partners in the pursuit of knowledge, understanding, and wisdom. A learning community is dedicated to educating the whole person—intellectual, spiritual, physical, and emotional essence. (pp. 12-13)

Pechman (1992) identifies eight common features of "educationally responsive schools" (p. 49), schools where approaches to teaching and learning reflect new understandings about cognition. These features include viewing learners as active constructors of meaning; utilizing a range of measures to evaluate progress and achievement; creating learning groups, around projects of interest, that are small, fluid, and personal and that allow students to collaborate in mixed-age groups and teams; developing interdisciplinary curricula that provide opportunities for students to study concepts in depth as opposed to memorizing facts or skimming over a multitude of ideas; and making significant connections between schools and home and community. Another feature of teaching and learning in PDSs is incorporating developing content standards into school curricula and using emerging standards of professional practice to inform decisions about who is permitted to teach and how instruction should be carried out. Valli (1994) writes of empowering learning communities in PDSs that are designed to emancipate learners from ignorance, trivial knowledge, subjugating knowledge, and hegemonic knowledge. Such learning communities are less bound to textbooks, teacher talk (e.g., lecturing), traditional grouping patterns, and the dominant culture. Their approaches to teaching and learning are constructivist, problem-focused, multicultural and inclusive, and social reconstructionist.

Rapid changes in the economy and the resulting demands on workers partly drive PDS emphasis on changing the content and methods of instruction ("A Conversation," 1997). Another compelling reason for shifting instructional paradigms toward more learner-centered practice is the need to accommodate the learning needs of an increasingly diverse student population ("Task Force on the Role," 1997). Culturally responsive practice has at its core a willingness to tailor instruction to the child instead of pinching and prodding the child to fit into a traditional, largely Eurocentric mold that many believe is fundamentally inadequate even for contemporary children from the majority culture.

In their review of PDS research literature, Valli, Cooper, and Frankes (1997) found only a few studies that documented student outcomes or indicated that more child-centered, constructivist, and cooperative instructional strategies are being tried in PDS settings. The literature reviews of Book (1996) and Teitel (1996) produced similar findings. In my review of project descriptions, I found that when classroom practices are discussed at all, more traditional structures and teacher-centered modes of instruction still prevail. For example, the insidious effects of tracking are well documented; lower tracks have characteristically been dumping grounds for low-achieving students, many of whom are from racial, ethnic, or linguistic minority groups (Lipman, 1997). However, despite a commitment to the principle of high expectations for all children and a stated objective to eliminate tracking, which often runs counter to this expectation, many partnerships appear to have been unable to restructure their schools to eliminate tracking. Webb-Dempsey's (1997) impact study of PDS programming in West Virginia cites the presence of vocational and college prep tracks in one high school PDS and notes the negative attitudes toward vocational students held by students from both tracks.

Several partnerships report that efforts to implement child-centered instruction that incorporates hands-on, active, constructivist approaches frequently meet with opposition from teachers and administrators (Morse, Daniels, & Flieg, 1995). Traditional student evaluation mechanisms often conflict with or ignore child-centered practices (Webb-Dempsey, 1997). In some school systems, teachers are required to "teach to the test," preparing students to pass district- or state-mandated standardized tests. Content and method are driven by these measures, and individual teachers often have little latitude in changing either. For example, a high school site coordinator at one of the AT&T Teachers for Tomorrow sites in New York recommended that student teachers not be placed in classrooms where seniors were preparing for New York state regents exams, primarily because teachers in such classes feel duty-bound to prepare students for the exams and are unwilling to deviate from the prescribed curriculum and methods (Abdal-Haqq, in press). Student teachers in PDSs, as well as other schools, frequently relate their frustration when they attempt culturally responsive practices or other nontraditional strategies or content (Lawrence, 1997; Wiseman & Cooner, 1996). Such resistance is often strongest in high schools because parents, as well as teachers and administrators, want students to be "ready" for the SAT or exit examinations and are unwilling to allow "experiments" at such a critical juncture in students' academic careers. Although traditional practices appear to prevail in PDSs, the literature is beginning to reveal glimpses of practice that reflects the child-centered concepts outlined earlier. Audiovisual material frequently provides vivid images of innovative practice in PDSs (Century Communications, 1996; NCREST, 1996).

Recent Research

THE PROFESSIONAL DEVELOPMENT SCHOOL STANDARDS PROJECT

Trachtman's (1996) survey of 28 partnerships found many sites attempting to create classroom environments characterized by "teaching for understanding" and "ambitious teaching." Children in these classrooms engaged in inquiry-based projects; utilized technology to generate knowledge; and engaged in new roles such as peer helper, caregiver, and self- and peer evaluator. Teachers are attempting to move from their conventional role of knowledge transmitters to knowledge facilitators. Teachers report moving from whole-class approaches to instructional approaches that focus on individual children and build on the children's prior experience and knowledge. Block scheduling has been implemented at one site; another site experimented with daily counseling-guidance seminars for ninth graders to increase student visibility and school retention; some sites have created multiage classrooms, which give teachers more opportunities to know students well because teacher and class stay together longer than 1 year. The presence of student teachers has provided more adult help and nurturing, enabling teachers to design more hands-on and out-of-classroom activities. More than 60% of the sites in Trachtman's study report significant use of state, local, and national standards. Although school faculty report that standardized testing remains in place, more than 70% of the sites are using multiple assessment mechanisms. Trachtman's respondents did not appear to have attempted systematic assessment of overall PDS effectiveness, but participants did claim successful outcomes. Some respondents noted significant improvements in standardized test scores, increased student self-esteem, more parental participation, and reduced suspensions and violence levels.

TEXAS A&M UNIVERSITY

Wiseman and Cooner (1996) describe a collaborative effort between university and elementary teachers to design a new model for presenting language arts methods to student teachers and to improve the writing proficiency of elementary students. In addition to staging on-site, weekly 3-hour lecture-discussion groups for student teachers and teachers, each of 125 university students became a "writing buddy" 1 additional hour a week for a small group of elementary students. Classroom teachers utilized the writing buddies in a variety of formats; one-to-one assistance or working with small groups of up to five children were common patterns. Students and teachers became enthusiastic about the program, and teacher participation grew from 80% in the first semester of the program to 100%. Over a 4-year period, the course design and the writing buddies program have been implemented at several schools, and the original site is experimenting with the format in a collaboratively taught technology course. The authors report that writing scores on the state achievement test increased from a 69% school pass rate to 82% after the first year and 92% after the second year.

The Houston Consortium of Urban Professional Development and Technology Centers (HCUPDTC)

A report on the PDSs involved in the HCUPDTC indicates that mathematics scores on the state achievement test increased in all 16 consortium PDSs, and reading scores increased in 14 of the 16 within 2 years of PDS implementation (Houston et al., 1995). The report suggests that this change is linked to one-to-one and small-group tutoring by preservice teachers who perform this task as part of their field-based methods coursework. Overall writing scores at the sites did not show similar improvement, which the authors attribute to the fact that tutoring in writing did not occur during the same period.

Although the report does not claim a causal relationship between a school's becoming a PDS and increases in student achievement, it does suggest that certain features of PDS activity may have contributed to improvements in student outcomes. The addition of interns and preinterns to classrooms lowered the student-adult ratio and provided children with greater access to adult mentoring, support, and instruction. Campus initiatives that included aligning curriculum with test objectives were also in place during the relevant period. In addition, consortium teachers engaged in professional development activities related to teaching in urban schools and the use of technology, and teachers and administrators worked collaboratively with university personnel to solve problems and share ideas. These factors, as well as being part of a new movement and the Hawthorne effect of change, may also have influenced achievement. The Houston Consortium's experience illustrates one difficulty in assessing the effectiveness of PDS programming: Without carefully designed evaluation mechanisms, it is often extremely difficult to isolate the impact of a single activity or set of activities when they occur in a setting awash with multiple initiatives.

THE BENEDUM COLLABORATIVE

Webb-Dempsey (1997) reports results of a comprehensive longitudinal assessment of the experiences of teachers and students in 5 of the 13 PDSs in the Benedum Collaborative, a partnership between West Virginia University and local schools. Multiple methodologies and multiple perspectives within those methodologies characterized the research design. Interview and survey data were gathered from students and from preservice and inservice teachers. Students were interviewed on site either individually or in small focus groups. To date, more than 400 PDS students have been interviewed by researchers, about 10% of the total PDS student population; more than 3,000 K-12 students were surveyed. State assessment data, including CTBS scores, were also incorporated into the analysis.

When findings from data collection were shared with site steering committees and other faculty groups, Webb-Dempsey reports that these findings spurred schools to action. For example, elementary students frequently reported distress as a result of "playground behaviors" that work against feelings of mutual respect and acceptance: name-calling, teasing, and the presence of cliques. African American elementary students displayed less positive feelings about themselves as successful students than other groups. Responses of both vocational-track students and college prep–track students were consistently negative about "vo-tech" students. These and other "red flag" issues provoked faculty strategizing and additional investigation to devise means of improving conditions for students.

An impressive aspect of the study's findings is the insight it provided into students' perceptions of how they learn best. "One-to-one" individualized instructional time with teachers and "hands-on" learning emerged across all responses as the most frequently cited beneficial instructional approaches. Students in one of the high schools that implemented a major structural change to a 90-minute block schedule overwhelmingly supported the change. The new schedule provided greater opportunity for cooperative learning, hands-on activities, critical-thinking learning experiences, and student-teacher interaction.

In a draft summary report on initial findings from the same study, Webb-Dempsey (n.d.) relates some of the CTBS student performance data collected for the five sites:

> In comparisons of the average mean percentile by school for all five PDSs, in all cases either the PDS is outperforming the WV [West Virginia] mean in a direct comparison or is improving at an accelerated rate relative to the state. In some schools both occur . . . [The data reveal] relative stability and/or improvement of CTBS [Comprehensive Tests of Basic Skills] mean percentile scores, even though the national trend in reforming schools is for scores to exhibit a "dip" or "J curve" during the first two to three years of a major reform effort. (p. 4)

Other examples of documented outcomes can be found in the PDS literature, although the majority of these examples do not emerge from systematic investigations like those cited above. Results are often embedded in case studies or project reports, or they are mentioned in fugitive literature sources. Unfortunately, the positive results that appear to have been occurring have not been adequately aggregated to form a comprehensive picture of PDS effectiveness.

In a case study that describes the PDS collaborative between Texas Tech University and local schools, Campbell, Strawderman, and Reavis (1996) report that teachers in the elementary PDS report stories of significant changes in the reading skills of students. The junior high PDS received district recognition for teacher and student school attendance improvements, and failure rates dropped from 18-20% in the years prior to PDS implementation to 11% for the last grading period. However, this information is presented in 5 lines embedded in an 11-page journal article, and no information is given about the explicit programming that brought about these outcomes.

In a report on the partnership between Michigan State University and its nine PDSs, Judge, Carriedo, and Johnson (1995) mention that math scores at one urban elementary PDS rose 45% over 4 years. The same report also describes an urban high school PDS in which fewer than 30% of ninth graders generally survive into the 10th grade. One significant group of these ninth graders worked with a team of ninth-grade teachers actively supported by university faculty, with the result that the persistence rate increased threefold during 1994. The authors also refer to an incident in which the university's president was told at a faculty meeting that much of the work on new state science assessment guidelines took place in a PDS. A review of the background material on the new guidelines substantiated this claim, but the published guidelines included no acknowledgment of the PDS. This last example provides a good example of one problem in identifying classroom-related work in PDSs. Accounts of such work often appear in other discipline-specific literature streams, such as math education or early childhood education. Frequently, neither the authors who report such work nor the abstractors who index the reports for education or social science databases recognize or consider it significant that the reported work takes place within a PDS context.

In general, the literature does not indicate that the majority of partnerships embedded in the development or implementation process a systematic, ongoing approach to documenting what was being done or evaluating the process or outcomes (Judge, Carriedo, & Johnson, 1995). Berry et al. (1996), in their examination of inquiry activity in PDSs, found few instances of baseline data being collected. Overall, such evaluative or descriptive studies as we have tend to reflect efforts to plunder archives or interview and/or survey participants in an effort to reconstruct events, an approach with inherent limitations (Clark, 1995). Those involved in this work are rightly skeptical about the appropriateness or adequacy of relying on standardized tests as the sole or primary measure of student achievement and development in PDS settings; however, there is little evidence in the literature to suggest that organized efforts have been undertaken to devise alternative methods that inspire confidence in their results.

Clark (1995), in discussing partner school evaluation, stresses the inappropriateness of relying on traditional research protocols, which are based on classic scientific methodology, to evaluate PDS work. Judge, Carriedo, and Johnson (1995) also point out that multiple measures, which include various forms of standardized testing, portfolio assessments, attendance information, dropout rates, report card grades, and teacher evaluation, should complement state-mandated achievement tests when evaluating PDS effects on students. The limits of traditional assessment measures and the challenges associated with devising new ones are also discussed by Webb-Dempsey (1997).

Inquiry in PDS Settings

The literature is less revealing about the nature of inquiry than it is about other aspects of PDSs, such as initial teacher preparation, professional development, collaboration, or governance (Valli, Cooper, & Frankes, 1997). However, there is reason to believe that collaborative research activity is taking place. In a 1994 survey of 66 partnerships, 81% of respondents indicated that collaborative research involving school and college faculty was a characteristic of the partnership (Abdal-Haqq, 1995b).

This review and personal communication with school and college faculty suggest that inquiry activities are taking place in PDSs, although the literature does not supply an organized portrait of either the nature of inquiry or its outcomes (Berry et al., 1996). For example, Troen and Bolles (1994) tell us that teachers in the Learning and Teaching Collaborative have one pupil-free day a week devoted to Alternative Professional Time. Teachers use this time for a variety of professional activities including research, but we do not get a clear picture of what they do and how they use their findings. The principal of an inner-city PDS in St. Louis described to me a successful action research project she under took to find out why so many of the elementary youngsters in her school were being suspended for misbehavior (S. Young, personal communication, February, 1996). As a result of her project, overall suspensions dropped dramatically in a few weeks; however, I have not run across an account of the project in the PDS literature.

Fugitive literature, particularly program newsletters, can be informative about inquiry activity in PDSs. For example, an issue of *Center Correspondent*, published by the Center for Educational Renewal (1995), featured summaries of inquiry projects conducted by members of an NNER Leadership Program cohort. Cohort members include principals and other school-based leaders who engage in yearlong inquiry into some aspect of the simultaneous renewal agenda. A recent issue of *PDS Proceedings* (1996), published by the University of South Carolina (USC), focused on inquiry activities of teachers and students in the USC PDS network. The newsletter announced winners of 11 PDS inquiry grants to school faculty teams and provided reports on several practice-oriented inquiry projects conducted by teachers. Although these reports are short on hard data, they do illustrate that PDS teachers are

1. Engaging in action research and other forms of inquiry
2. Achieving positive results
3. Using their findings to inform their practice

Four Cities Urban PDS Network is a newsletter published by the University of Wisconsin—Milwaukee. The first issue (1995) reported on inquiry projects focusing on reducing behavior-related disturbances and behavior referrals at an urban elementary school. School-based research on curriculum issues (e.g., integrating African American history and culture; incorporating knowledge about urban families and communities into teacher education curriculums) was also reported in the newsletter.

3

Finding Time, Finding Money

This chapter examines two problematic nuts-and-bolts issues that plague PDS development and implementation: time and financing. In its draft standards for professional development schools, the PDS Standards Project (Levine, 1996b) outlines two levels of standards: threshold conditions and quality standards. Institutional commitment by both partners of financial and human resources to the PDS is one of the threshold conditions; adequate time to do the work is one indicator that this particular threshold condition is being met. Although the PDS literature is fairly expansive in its documentation of the processes and structures associated with collaborative decision making—another threshold condition—discussions about time and financial constraints more often than not consist of lamentations and war stories. However, the literature is beginning to provide reports of systematic efforts to document how partnerships are coping with the seemingly chronic lack of time and to identify costs and devise efficient funding.

Finding Time

Planning and implementing a professional development school in all its facets is generally acknowledged to be a very labor-intensive enterprise that requires considerable investments of time by school and university faculty, as well as student interns. In addition to some obvious things that consume time (e.g., coursework, consultations, conducting research), constructing the interpersonal infrastructure necessary for successful partnering also requires significant amounts of time. This work involves what Ariav and Clinard (1996) define as "building trust and developing collaborative dialogue" and "establishing communications links" (p. 11). Time devoted to trust building and developing shared understandings can be critical in the formative stages of a partnership (Bell, 1995). The strains on participants sometimes result in burnout and dropping out, and the prospect of time demands sometimes leads faculty and students to opt out of participation (Abdal-Haqq, in press). In general, the literature provides more information about arrangements designed to facilitate school faculty participation than it does about what is being done to ease the burden on preservice teachers or college faculty.

Time constraints on teachers who are active in PDS work can be considerable. Although the work frequently engages teachers in new roles and assignments, most teachers typically do not receive consistent release time for these noninstructional tasks. A national survey found that only about 10% of the PDSs provided reduced course loads for mentor, master, or cooperating teachers, and only 25% provided release time (Abdal-Haqq, 1995b). Consequently, time must be found outside of the school day or squeezed from odd hours within it.

The proliferation of school reform initiatives over the last decade has increased demands on teacher time nationwide; PDS teachers are not alone in this regard. A report by the National Education Commission on Time and Learning (NECTL), *Prisoners of Time*, indicates that what teachers are expected to know and do has increased in amount and complexity (NECTL, 1994). Bull, Buechler, Didley, and Krehbiel (cited in Abdal-Haqq, 1996b) point out that meeting the demands that come from redefining teacher work may be particularly stressful for America's aging teaching force, which averages 14.5 years of service. The majority of these teachers received their training at a time when teaching did not routinely require many of the pedagogical or noninstructional skills that are needed to function effectively in restructured, learner-centered schools. Teachers need time to understand new concepts; learn new skills; develop new attitudes; research, discuss, reflect, assess, try new approaches and integrate them into their practice; and plan their own professional development (Abdal-Haqq, 1996b; Troen & Bolles, 1994; Watts & Castle, 1993).

A major theme in the NECTL report (1994) is that both students and teachers in American schools are victims of inflexible and counterproductive schedules. Structural arrangements that facilitate active, cooperative, learner-centered practice are not widespread, nor is accommodation normally made within the school schedule for consulting or observing colleagues or engaging in professional activities such as research, learning and practicing new skills, curriculum development, or professional reading. Administrators, parents, and legislators typically view unfavorably anything that draws teachers away from the classroom during school hours (Trachtman, 1996). Indeed, teachers themselves often feel guilty about being away from their classrooms for restructuring or staff development activities (Abdal-Haqq, 1996b).

Growing recognition of the importance of providing teachers with opportunities to collaborate, plan, and engage in noninstructional professional work has led researchers to investigate what schools and school districts are doing to redesign schedules to accommodate new patterns and approaches to teaching and learning (NECTL, 1994; Watts & Castle, 1993). In a study of regional and national innovative school groups, Raywid (cited in Abdal-Haqq, 1996b) found three broad approaches to finding time for teachers to collaborate:

1. Adding time by extending the school day
2. Extracting time from the existing schedule
3. Altering staff utilization patterns

Watts and Castle's (1993) survey of schools involved in National Education Association initiatives revealed five types or categories of time created for the kinds of teacher development and collaborative activities that typically take place in PDSs:

- *Freed-up time:* for example, using teaching assistants, college interns, parents, and administrators to cover classes; regular early release days
- *Restructured or rescheduled time:* for example, lengthening the school day for 4 days, with an early release on Day 5
- *Better-used time:* for example, using regular staff or district meetings for planning and professional growth rather than for informational or administrative purposes
- *Common time:* for example, scheduling common planning periods for colleagues having similar assignments
- *Purchased time:* for example, establishing a substitute bank of 30-40 days per year that teachers can tap when they want to participate in committee work or professional development activities

The PDS literature documents several instances of teachers in PDSs finding more time for professional development, supervision, and collaborative work through one of these approaches. For example, Troen and Bolles (1994) describe an innovative variation of freed-up time where teachers have at least one pupil-free day a week to pursue professional interests or alternative roles. The presence of team teaching and full-time teacher interns who can take over classes enables this approach to work. About half of the respondents in Trachtman's (1996) survey of 28 PDS sites revealed that the presence of student teachers permitted teachers to engage in professional development activities during the school day. The national trend to experiment with block scheduling can also yield dividends for school faculty who need time for noninstructional activities (Abdal-Haqq, 1996b). PDS literature indicates that sites are involved in efforts to implement block schedules as part of general school renewal efforts (Saab, Steel, & Shive, 1997; Trachtman, 1996; Webb-Dempsey, 1997). Grant funds often supply the means to purchase substitutes, enabling teachers to engage in work related to student intern supervision, collaborative planning, or attending or conducting courses (Abdal-Haqq, in press; Vaughn, 1996).

In profiles of seven partner schools within the NNER, Vaughn (1996) found that although each category of making time noted by

Watts and Castle (1993) was employed in at least one of the seven partner schools surveyed, the first, freed-up time, was the most prevalent. For example, in one of the surveyed schools, community volunteers taught enrichment classes in arts and crafts, sports, and other areas once a week—freeing teachers for planning, collaboration, and parent-teacher conferences. Vaughn's findings reflect the general trend found in PDS literature: Structural innovations that create time to perform tasks associated with school renewal, teacher development, or inquiry are more likely to endure when they do not require significant outlays of financial resources by school districts or do not depend on short-term grant funding. Reallocation of existing resources, both human and financial, and tapping nontraditional sources for classroom substitutes appear to be the cost-effective methods of choice.

The literature on time also reflects a principle associated with PDSs by the Holmes Group (1986)—PDSs are context based. Sites have devised a number of diverse approaches to giving school faculty the time they need to implement programming, and these approaches reflect the unique character, resources, and requirements of the schools that implement them. Crawford et al. (1993) describe how one clinical professor at a PDS affiliated with Indiana State University acted as a substitute, enabling teachers to participate in the school's restructuring committee. Williams (1996) writes that PDS sites in the Indiana State University partnership are required to commit 50% of their professional development resources to program goals. Because the sites receive no public funds for professional development, they humorously offered to commit all such resources to the partnership. Knowing that each school had a contractual obligation to hold monthly faculty meetings, partnership organizers asked that at least half of the meeting be devoted to PDS planning and discussion; the targeted resource was time. To reduce school faculty burnout, some partnerships allow teachers who work with interns to take "sabbaticals" from active PDS work or to choose less time-consuming levels of involvement, such as receiving preinterns for occasional observation or demonstrations, and some partnerships rotate sites to relieve the strain (Abdal-Haqq, in press).

More intense supervision and on-site work can be extremely taxing for university-based faculty as well, particularly in cases where significant distances are involved and standard course loads are not reduced. About 70% of respondents in a national survey of 66 partnerships indicated that they provide release time or reduced load for college faculty involved in PDS work. Clustering teacher education students for fieldwork at a few sites and holding classes on site—to save travel time—are the most prevalent accommodations to university faculty needs (Hausfather, Outlaw, & Strehle, 1996; Hecht, Bland, Schoon, & Boschert, 1996).

Compared to traditional practicums, field-based programs in PDSs are generally longer and involve more interaction between the student and college and school personnel. Low-income students, mature students with families, and others who must work may find these demands burdensome. Some partnerships are experimenting with individualized programs (Martin, 1996), distance learning schemes (Osguthorpe et al., 1995), part-time programs (Houston et al., 1995), and electronic networks (Hausfather, Outlaw, & Strehle, 1996; Houston et al., 1995; Newman et al., 1996) to make it easier for students to participate in the PDS preservice program.

Although the literature does document several cases in which PDSs have developed and refined promising structural arrangements related to the issue of time, in general there appears to be either a precarious reliance on purchasing time with grant funds or an apologetic and resigned acceptance that PDS work is an add-on that requires sacrifices of personal and professional time by school and university teachers. Similarly, PDS literature does not indicate that there is widespread attention to the needs of working teacher education students or those whose domestic situations limit the amount of time they can devote to fieldwork or to a certification program. Resolution of the time problem has implications for PDS commitment to equity, given that junior faculty in universities, many of whom are female, are disproportionately represented in field-based work and that many of the low-income and working-class teacher education students are from racial or ethnic minority groups. Thus, finding time for all participants to do the work becomes a matter of both pragmatism and principle.

Financing

A persistent theme in PDS literature is the difficulty of finding funds to develop and sustain programs. In general, the literature suggests that partnerships find it easier to acquire developmental funds than maintenance support. Clark and Plecki (1997) indicate that one of the problems in securing funds for PDSs may be the lack of sufficient information about costs and the resulting inability to accurately compare costs across sites because of different organizational arrangements and accounting methods. The literature provides few data and reflects relatively little systematic inquiry into the cost of operating a PDS. For several years, three papers by Theobold (cited in Clark & Plecki, 1997), published in 1990 and 1991, and a 1992 paper on costs and benefits by Harris (cited in Arends & Winitzky, 1996) were about the only readily available works on costs. A recently published work by Clark (1997) of the NNER provides what may be the most detailed explication to date of PDS start-up and maintenance costs. Using data collected from 18 NNER partner schools, Clark outlines typical start-up costs and provides two cost models illustrating how operating costs might be reasonably distributed between partners. The study suggests that start-up costs average $50,000 over a 2-year period and that once start-up costs have been met, school renewal and teacher education functions in PDSs can be covered through reallocation of existing levels of university and school district funding.

Clark and Plecki (1997) identify six budget categories to which resources needed for PDS work can be assigned: one-time expenditures or start-up costs, marginal costs, opportunity costs, indirect costs, joint funding and in-kind contributions, and intangible resources. Ishler and Edens (1995) and others (Hecht et al., 1996; Houston et al., 1995) acknowledge that field-based programs are generally more expensive to operate than campus-based programs. Theobald (cited in Clark, 1997) estimates that costs for schools and universities may increase by as much as 10%. Costs can vary considerably across sites because of the nature of the program. For example, Warner (1996) discusses how current funding formulas for state institutions may be inadequate to support technology-intensive field-based teacher education programs. Where do the partners get the money to support programming? Clark's (1997) investigation showed that successful PDSs typically employ one of four approaches to financing:

1. Eliminate old programs and redirect funds to PDSs
2. Jointly commit to sharing developmental and operating costs
3. Obtain substantial funding from external sources
4. Adopt an "entrepreneurial approach" (p. 14), which may combine the first three with additional creative touches

For example, the Houston Consortium has combined approaches 2 and 3; although grant funds provided partial support for systematic redesign of the existing programs, the nine institutions in the consortium committed themselves to continue the program regardless of external funding, relying on tuition and regular state or private funding for support (Houston et al., 1995). Bullough, Jr. et al. (1997b) indicate that tenure-track lines in the department budget were reallocated to clinical faculty hired for field-based work. In his review of PDS literature, Teitel (1996) found several creative approaches to financing among sites but an overall shortage of systematic attention to financing and funding sources.

In a 1994 survey of 66 partnerships, about 52% of the respondents reported receiving funds from school districts, 71% received college funds, and almost 64% received funds from foundations and other private sources. Of the 71% that received college funds, 63% reported that these funds were, at least in part, "soft money" (Abdal-Haqq, 1995b).

Although the PDS literature is not particularly explicit about what it costs to operate individual programs, a review of project reports and descriptions does suggest that the preponderance of programs are on shaky ground financially because they rely on public and private grants or discretionary funds, particularly for start-up costs (Darling-Hammond, 1994). State (Williams, 1996) and federal block grants for specific initiatives have been used to support PDSs. Eisenhower professional development funds

(Abdal-Haqq, in press), National Endowment for the Humanities grants (Anderson et al., 1995), and Title VII bilingual education (Le-Compe, Irby, & Lara-Alecio, 1995) and Title I (Century Communications, 1996) funds are among the federal sources cited in the literature.

In cases where PDS programming has been institutionalized to a degree, grant funds, although short-lived, have been instrumental in supporting initial efforts long enough to produce results that were sufficiently impressive to induce partner institutions to provide line-item funds for some PDS components. This has been the case with some of the Teachers for Tomorrow projects funded by the AT&T Foundation (Abdal-Haqq, in press). The literature documents other cases in which start-up grants enabled partnerships to establish themselves sufficiently to attract grant funds from other sources (Abdal-Haqq, in press; Houston et al., 1995).

Reallocation of existing funds is often the most realistic alternative, given the improbability of sufficient amounts of public school or university funds becoming available. There appears to be a general consensus in the literature that PDSs are doomed to early extinction as long as they are regarded as add-ons to regular school or university programming (Ishler & Edens, 1995; Sykes, 1997). The task is to provide credible evidence and convincing arguments that PDS settings perform functions that each partner values at an attractive price—that is, the PDS can do the job less expensively or give greater value for the money invested.

4

Professional Development Schools and School Reform

Three broad initiatives associated with school restructuring and reform have significant practical and philosophical implications for PDS programming: parent involvement, integrated services, and technology infusion. Whether and how these initiatives are being merged with teacher education and school renewal activities are important for two reasons. First, each appears to be compatible with one or more of the primary goals associated with the PDS mission. Second, each seems to be on an inexorable path toward becoming a meaningful element in public schooling. Thus, if PDSs take seriously their mission of preparing effective educators for tomorrow's schools, as well as testing and refining productive practices, then attention to these initiatives becomes both a duty and necessity. This chapter summarizes the major benefits of parent involvement, integrated services, and technology infusion and examines what the literature reports about the extent to which PDS programming incorporates each initiative.

Parent Involvement

During the last few years, several high-profile initiatives designed to increase parent and community involvement in the education and welfare of children have been launched. The largest, Partnership for Family Involvement in Education, is sponsored by the U.S. Department of Education (DOE; n.d.). Its mission is to promote children's learning through family-school-community partnerships. In 1996, researchers at Johns Hopkins University established the National Network of Partnership-2000 Schools, which is designed to bring together schools, districts, and states that are committed to developing and maintaining strong school-family-community partnerships (*Type 2*, 1996). In January, the National PTA (1997) announced publication of a handbook that highlights six standards designed to bolster parent involvement in education. The standards were developed in cooperation with the National Coalition for Parent Involvement in Education. The National PTA was instrumental in adding parent involvement to the original six, now eight, National Education Goals: "Every school will promote partnerships that will increase parental involvement and participation in promoting the social, emotional and academic growth of children" (National PTA, 1997, p. 1).

The literature on the benefits of parent involvement for schools, children, and families is extensive and compelling. Among other findings, research shows that regardless of socioeconomic status, ethnic or racial background, or parents' education level, students achieve at higher levels when parents are involved in their children's education (National PTA, 1997). The DOE report, *Strong Families, Strong Schools* (cited in Carey & Farris, 1996), indicates that children earn higher grades and test scores and remain in school longer when parents are actively involved in children's learning; parents influence learning most significantly through the attitudes, values, and materials found in the home environment; and significant levels of parent involvement in a school improves the performance of all children in the school. (See Buttery and Anderson [1997] for a concise synthesis of literature on parent-school-community dynamics.)

Overall, the literature suggests that explicit programming to involve parents and communities in developing and implementing PDS work is not widespread (Valli, Cooper, & Frankes, 1997; Zeichner & Miller, 1997). Reported instruction and activities appear to be fairly conventional and superficial. The most common type of parent involvement seems to be parent participation on site or multisite steering committees, but the literature reveals little about how parents influence these committees. Given the extensive body of research supporting the efficacy of parent involvement and teacher familiarity with students' families and communities (Kendall, 1993; McLaughlin, 1994; Nieto, 1992), particularly with regard to children from historically disadvantaged groups, the relatively low level and intensity of PDS family-community programming is somewhat disturbing.

Nevertheless, PDS literature does include some examples of sites that are experimenting with innovative ways to bring families, schools, teacher education students, and university faculty together in mutually beneficial ways. Webb-Dempsey (1997) indicates that parents were involved in designing the Benedum Collaborative's assessment of PDS impact. LeCompe, Irby, and Lara-Alecio (1995) describe a community learning activity based at an elementary PDS affiliated with Sam Houston State University in Houston. The Saturday School at Sammons (SSS) is a 10-week Saturday program for parents and children that involves ESL classes, computer training, and employment support services for parents. The parent education component is based on an assessment of community needs, and the involvement of preservice teachers and school and college faculty who work daily with children in the program offers a natural venue for opening up family-school communication.

Lancy (1997) describes an effort to involve parents in the work of an urban high school PDS that has significant numbers of special education students and students considered vulnerable to school failure. Although results were mixed, an important lesson emerged: Parents are more likely to endorse and support school change initiatives when they can clearly discern tangible benefits for their children. A seven-member parent leadership team was formed in a Detroit PDS to identify problems and needs within the school and to work with other parents to find solutions (Alber, 1995). Members of the team participated in group process training, organized schoolwide parent workshops, launched school improvement projects, and eventually formed a parent advocacy group designed to take parent concerns to the state level.

Barriers to parent involvement in PDSs differ very little from barriers in other schools (Alber, 1995). They include overt or tangible impediments such as transportation difficulties, burdensome work schedules, or language barriers. They also include assumptions on the part of school personnel that parents are too ignorant or too indifferent to make meaningful partners in children's education (Kendall, 1993). Parents too have their assumptions, which may be based on past negative experiences with school personnel, an expectation that they will be patronized or stonewalled, or a belief that direct involvement in school decision making is not their purview.

I recall a story related by a university faculty member who described efforts to actively involve parents in school renewal activities at an urban PDS. The site committee that convened a parent meeting was forcefully admonished by a small but vocal set of parents who considered that they were being asked to involve themselves in making decisions that teachers were paid to make. In my opinion, the moral of this story is not that some people are too ignorant to take advantage of opportunities that are presented to them. The moral is that PDSs, like other schools, need to (1) devise strategies that offer parents multiple points of entry into the school experiences of their children; and (2) recognize that parents support children's learning in intangible ways that may not be obvious (Buttery & Anderson, 1997; Nieto, 1992).

In learner-centered schools, children are encouraged to develop responsibility, in ways that are meaningful to them, for their own learning and that of their peers. A foundation is laid for participation as citizens in a democratic society. In learner-centered school communities, every parent does not have to sit on a committee, bake cookies, or coach a softball team, but every parent has a responsibility to his or her own child and to other children in the school community. Parent involvement research shows that what parents do in their homes, churches, and neighborhoods can positively affect the learning of their children and other children in the school (Carey & Farris, 1996; National PTA, 1997; Nieto, 1992). PDS implementers can advance their school renewal agendas by redefining the boundaries of the school and expanding them to incorporate the larger community; challenging parents, families, and communities to promote the academic and social development of students; and developing structures and approaches that make meaningful family and community involvement possible.

Integrated Services

Integrated services programs, also known as comprehensive services, are proactive approaches to addressing the multiple needs of children and families. Because schools are the places where children tend to be most readily available on a regular basis for sustained, predictable time periods, the school becomes the hub of an interlocking network of school-based or school-linked services and resources that focus on prevention, treatment, and support. These programs bring together education, human service, health, employment, mental health, social work, and juvenile justice professionals in a coordinated effort to promote the welfare of children and their families (*School-Linked Comprehensive Services*, 1995).

Such programs may provide various combinations of the following services and programs: job counseling and location services for teens and adults; gang and teen pregnancy prevention; counseling and support for adjudicated youth; primary health care for students and families; day care and parenting, health, and nutrition resources for teen parents; GED and adult education for family members; mental health counseling; dropout prevention; and substance abuse prevention. Case management is a common approach to service delivery in such programs. Although integrated services programs are commonly driven by concerns about at-risk or vulnerable children and youth (Bucci & Reitzammer, 1992; Lawson, 1996) they are essentially an approach to promoting wellness and achievement for all students.

Incorporating integrated services concepts into PDS programming is mentioned in several discussions of PDS principles and implementation strategies (Ishler & Edens, 1995; Kozleski et al., 1997; Murray, 1993; "Vision Statement," 1993). However, the literature supplies few examples of interprofessional collaboration within PDS partnerships (Teitel, 1996).

Osguthorpe et al. (1995) include in their descriptions of the 15 partnerships in the NNER site descriptions of three partnerships that have interprofessional collaboration components. A major component of the Texas Educational Collaborative is "family and home connections" (p. 305), which involve counselors, administrators, health and human service workers, adult literacy workers, teachers, and university personnel. Eight adults from among these groups, as well as student teachers and community volunteers, work in family groups that include 25 children. "Families" meet each week, and each adult establishes a personal relationship with three to four children. Wright State University (OH) has implemented a Partners Transforming Education collaboration, intended to become a learning laboratory for "rethinking and restructuring professional development in education and human services at Wright State University while simultaneously engaging in the renewal of schools and human services agencies" (p. 307). The Institute for Educational Renewal (IER) at Miami University (OH) includes health and human service agencies, as well as schools, in the partnership. It focuses on collaborative interprofessional approaches to strengthening education and services for children and families and strengthening preservice and inservice professional development of school and human service personnel.

With support from the DeWitt Wallace-Reader's Digest Fund, the University of Louisville implemented an interdisciplinary professional development and service delivery model, which involves seven university units or disciplines, three public schools, and two on-site Youth Service Centers. Known as the Wellness Project, this program has launched several projects reflecting local needs, including peer mediation, family education resources for teen parents, immunization, and legal education for parents, students, and teachers. The projects involve preservice students in service delivery. The Wellness Project has also produced three cases for use in case-based interdisciplinary seminars, as well as a video about the seminars (*The Professional Development Community*, 1994). Lawson, et al. (1995) advise PDSs to expand the concept of partnership to make it more relevant to the needs of vulnerable children and families:

> Reform of schools and teacher education alone, though making important strides in many areas, does not go far enough in serving children in areas where poverty, crime, and other societal problems are located in school communities. Instead of being considered school system challenges, children's needs, problems, and aspirations may be recast as family support/empowerment and community development issues. . . . Expanded partnerships cultivate support and empowerment networks for children and families. They mobilize parents, agencies, and services to address constraints and barriers to children's learning, development, and health. The partners band together on partner school sites (school-based services) or near these sites (school-linked services). They invite professionals from education and human services into the community to discuss and plan for educational renewal. The agenda that began with school reform is thus expanded to include organizational restructuring, cross-system collaboration, family support, and community development. The intended result is the *transformation* of the organizations and systems that serve children and families. (p. 213)

Expanding school-university partnerships to include human services and community agencies requires that both partners address three areas of teacher development: changing preservice and inservice teachers' attitudes about teacher roles, extending their knowledge of human services, and developing collaborative skills (Bucci & Reitzammer, 1992). Other considerations include assessment venues that reflect redesigned interdisciplinary curricula and expanded notions of appropriate field placements (Lawson, 1996; Lawson et al., 1995).

Technology Infusion

Whereas parent involvement walked into prominence with a steady tread and dogged persistence, and integrated services seems to be coming to the fore on crepe soles, technology infusion has stomped its way into America's schools with all the noise and glitz of someone wearing rhinestone cowboy boots. Of the three reform initiatives discussed in this chapter, technology infusion is the most widely documented in the PDS literature. Some partnerships have their origins in state-funded technology initiatives (Warner, 1996).

Several factors have conspired to produce the expectation and, in some cases, the requirement that teachers be able to utilize instructional technology, particularly computer-based technologies. These factors include the following:

1. The need to provide relevant, authentic instruction that reflects contemporary and future social and economic demands
2. The compatibility of certain computer-based technologies with newer, research-based approaches to teaching and learning
3. Student and parent expectations
4. Guidelines and mandates from federal, state, district, and professional bodies. (Abdal-Haqq, 1995a; "A Conversation," 1997; Cummins & Sayers, 1995; Pechman, 1992)

Drucker (cited in Conroy, Jensen, Bainbridge, & Catron, 1996) describes the importance of computer technology in the learning environment and how it affects the teacher's role.

There are more hours of pedagogy in one thirty-second commercial than most teachers can pack into a month of teaching. The subject matter of the TV commercial is quite secondary; what matters is the skill, professionalism, and persuasive power of presentation. Children, therefore, come to school today with expectations that are bound to be disappointed and frustrated. They expect a level of teaching competence that goes beyond what most teachers can possibly muster. Schools will increasingly be forced to use computers, television, films, videotapes, and audio tapes. The teacher increasingly will become a supervisor and mentor. . . . The teacher's job will be to help, to lead, to set examples, to encourage; it may not primarily be to convey the subject matter itself. (p. 15)

Despite increased numbers of computers in schools, according to the Office of Technology Assessment (1995), relatively few teachers routinely use computer-based technologies for instructional purposes; when computers are used, they are generally used for relatively low-level tasks such as drills and word processing; and computers are not sufficiently integrated across the curriculum. The most common reasons given for low levels of computer use are limited access to equipment and lack of training, particularly in more sophisticated applications such as multimedia and presentation packages, electronic networks, or problem-solving applications (Abdal-Haqq, 1995a). Critics of teacher education charge that

1. Teacher educators do not sufficiently model appropriate instructional use of computers in coursework or in the field
2. Technology is typically not incorporated across the teacher education curriculum
3. Preservice and inservice instruction tends to focus more on older and simpler applications and less on newer, more sophisticated applications that support development of higher-order thinking and problem-solving skills (Abdal-Haqq, 1995a)

Partnerships are infusing technology into programs in several ways. In Wyoming, where a partner school may be 300 miles from the university, interactive compressed video is used to conduct meetings and deliver some graduate level classes (Kleinsasser & Paradis, 1997). Gallaudet University has tried similar distance-learning vehicles to facilitate its individualized, part-time teacher education program (Martin, 1996). E-mail, listservs, and other telecommunications applications are the most common uses of computer technology (Hecht et al., 1996; Houston et al., 1995; Newman et al., 1996). PDS literature also includes reports of teachers using computer technology to enhance student learning experiences, including some "high level" applications (DeWert & Cory, 1996; Newman et al., 1996; Trachtman, 1996).

Lack of training, inadequate equipment, and insufficient access plague PDS partners as they do other schools and universities (American Association of Colleges for Teacher Education, 1995; Hecht et al., 1996; Persichitte, Tharp, & Cafferella, 1997). Several partnerships have upgraded their technology infrastructure and have incorporated technology topics into their preservice and in-service professional development programs for teachers, as well as faculty development for university personnel (Houston et al., 1995; Newman et al., 1996).

Technology infusion across the curriculum does not appear to be widespread in either schools or SCDEs involved in PDSs. Isolated coursework seems to be the pattern in teacher education programs. In schools, incorporating technology into instruction or cocurricular activities appears to be a matter of individual teacher initiative. Greater integration, more proficient teachers, and widespread usage are more prevalent in schools involved in federal, state, or privately funded technology initiatives. Overall, the literature suggests that PDSs are conforming to general trends related to technology infusion rather than setting new ones.

5

Voices of Caution: Equity Issues

In PDS literature, virtually every statement of mission, principles, goals and objectives, or commitments includes some reference to equity. Equity is a multidimensional issue in PDSs, as it is in schools and universities generally. It relates not only to expectations, attitudes, curriculum, and practice for children from low-income or racial, ethnic, and linguistic minority groups but also to staffing patterns, relationships between partners, program emphasis, recruitment and admissions policies, governance structures, sources of knowledge and expertise, and distribution of resources (Teitel, 1996; Valli, Cooper, & Frankes, 1997). Diversity is a term frequently used interchangeably with equity in the literature. In her discussion of how professional development schools might make concrete their vision of learning communities, Valli (1994) gives an example of how members of such communities might advance their equity and social justice agenda by becoming less bound to the dominant culture:

> Members would be encouraged to study diversity not merely as cultural differences to be respected, but as differences created by power relationships. Students would examine what keeps certain groups "from freely enjoying the social and financial rewards" of the country while other groups dominate and benefit. (p. 19)

This chapter looks at what the literature tells us about the extent to which equity or diversity-related programming and practices in PDS settings reflect examination of unequal power relationships

between and within schools and universities and between historically dominated groups and schools, universities, and the larger
society. As mentioned above, equity issues cut across multiple facets of the enterprise of schooling, and the literature confirms its
ubiquity in PDS settings. This chapter does not attempt to discuss
equity in relation to all, or even most, of these aspects of PDS programming; it primarily focuses on two broad categories—teacher
development and student learning.

In their review of PDS research literature, Valli, Cooper, and
Frankes (1997) assert that the PDS represents a particular vision of
change. They examine documented changes in PDS settings
through the lens of equity and categorize the changes noted as
first- or second-order changes. First-order changes are "intended to
make existing organizational goals and structures more efficient and
effective. They are solutions to quality control problems" (p. 253).
Second-order changes, in contrast,

> restructure the organization itself. As solutions to design prob-
> lems, they "introduce new goals, structures, and roles, that
> transform familiar ways of doing things into new ways of solv-
> ing persistent problems. . . . [They are] attempts to fundamen-
> tally alter existing authority, roles, and uses of time and space."
> (p. 253)

My review of the literature suggests that PDSs, on the whole,
have made more progress in bringing about second-order changes
in teacher education than in the context and content of P–12 teaching and student learning. However, even in teacher development,
fundamental changes have not been widespread in some areas.

The most significant progress can be seen in the almost univer-
sal attempt to shift from a university-dominated teacher education
model to one that acknowledges, values, and incorporates the knowledge that schools and teachers possess and generate. PDSs have
labored intensely to develop communication links and structures
to ensure that preservice and inservice teacher development is a
collaborative enterprise in PDS settings (Teitel, 1997a). Judge, Carriedo, and Johnson (1995) stress that "the PDS is to be, first and fore-
most, a partnership and not a colonising effort by the university"

(p. 2). Commitment to parity among partners, a principle that is as omnipresent in the literature as the commitment to equity, has received concentrated attention. PDS theorists and practitioners have examined the historical inequities between universities and schools and have attempted to alter the traditional power relationship. They have focused attention on the question of whose knowledge counts (Bullough, Jr. et al., 1997a; Collinson et al., 1994), identified traditional answers to the question, and set about trying to broaden the knowledge base for teacher education by incorporating knowledge articulated and generated by school-based practitioners. Of course, the extent to which the power balance has actually shifted varies from setting to setting.

A number of authors have pointed out that the trappings of collaboration and reflective practice may conceal a business-as-usual reality (Meyers, 1996; Zeichner, 1992). School improvement and organizational change literature reminds us that educational institutions are notoriously resistant to change (Fullan, 1995). Nevertheless, if we look at PDS achievements related to parity, we find that they reflect attempts to examine prevailing inequitable power relationships and devise mechanisms to bring about a more equitable realignment. The issue is not so much whether they have succeeded, but whether their attempts to bring about parity have incorporated critical analysis of values, priorities, and the political dynamics of existing relationships.

Some progress also has been made in altering the pattern of teacher development from a skills-driven, top-down, idiosyncratic format to a model that is more systematic and more influenced by individual needs and the contexts in which teachers work. Teacher development in PDSs is more likely to encourage inquiry and reflection and provide opportunities for teachers to construct knowledge rather than be passive recipients of it (Lieberman & Miller, 1992). Definitions of teacher work have been broadened in PDSs to incorporate new leadership roles. The result, as discussed in Chapter 1, is that both preservice and inservice teachers report greater feelings of empowerment, self-efficacy, and professional growth in PDSs. How lasting these changes are; the degree to which new orientations, experiences, and skills are transferrable to non-PDS settings; and most important, whether these changes translate into improvements in student outcomes remain largely unanswered questions in the PDS literature. After all, as Zeichner and Miller (1997) remind us, a more reflective teacher is not necessarily more effective.

However, these changes do represent fundamental redefinitions of how teachers should be prepared, the skills they need to be effective, and the degree of control they should have over what and how they learn. As such, they do reflect altered views about goals, authority, and power, and more important, they reflect focused attention by programmers on the power relations that have traditionally characterized teacher development.

PDS literature does not suggest that an equal degree of attention has been focused on promoting diversity in the teaching force or preparing teachers to engage in more culturally responsive practice (Zeichner & Miller, 1997). In fact, certain structural characteristics of preservice preparation tend to make it harder for low-income and working-class students, many of whom are from historically disadvantaged or dominated groups, to participate in PDS programs than in conventional programs. Field experiences tend to be longer and more time-consuming in PDSs, and programs are more likely to involve postbaccalaureate internships. This extra time may be so burdensome for working students or students who have to start earning as soon as possible that they are forced to opt out or drop out of PDS programs (Abdal-Haqq, in press).

If, as a number of authors have noted (Darling-Hammond, 1994; Levine, 1996a; Minnesota State Board of Teaching, 1994), these institutions are intended to become the sole gateway into the profession, PDSs may simply reinforce existing patterns of power and privilege. The well-off and the white will be admitted to the profession in large numbers; the poor and students of color will be underrepresented. The prevailing imbalance in the teaching force—that is, the percentage of racial, ethnic, and linguistic minority students is increasing while the percentage of teachers from these groups is decreasing or not keeping pace (*Task Force*, 1997)—will be reinforced. PDSs also tend to have more stringent admissions criteria than conventional programs, including acceptable scores on standardized tests. The pass rates on these tests for minority students are generally lower than for their peers, and this differential performance may also reduce minority group admittance to PDS programs (Abdal-Haqq, in press).

Although cultural congruence is not a guarantee of effective teaching, diversity literature does confirm that it has important advantages for minority group students. In addition, a diverse teaching force benefits all children and professional educators because it exposes them to different perspectives and provides them with opportunities to expand their views about who has the power that comes from knowledge and skill (Abdal-Haqq, 1994; Nieto, 1992). PDS literature does supply a few examples of attempts to recruit and retain low- and moderate-income students and students from underrepresented groups. Strategies include coaching and tutoring for entry exams; diversifying admissions assessment; developing part-time or individualized practicums; and providing or arranging stipends, paid internships, or employment as substitutes or paraprofessionals (Abdal-Haqq, in press; Martin, 1996; Minnesota State Board of Teaching, 1994).

An additional concern related to equity is the capacity of partnerships and the sources that fund them to support a sufficient number of PDSs to provide clinical sites for the number of teachers needed. What happens to students who cannot obtain a place in a PDS, particularly if states begin to require PDS internships for certification? Will those with the strongest credentials and the greatest means have preference? The PDS literature is virtually silent on this issue.

With regard to PDS programming designed to prepare teachers who are culturally responsive practitioners, PDS literature, overall, suggests that such programming has relatively little depth. There are accounts of PDSs making a concerted effort to place student teachers in schools with diverse student populations. There are also references to preservice and inservice coursework that focuses on multicultural education and diversity issues. What is not equally evident is whether the content and focus of this coursework or field placements are designed to challenge underlying assumptions that govern how schools are structured, who controls them, their purpose, how they relate to students and families, and how they support societal inequities (McCarthy, cited in Abdal-Haqq, 1994; Meyers, 1996; Zeichner & Miller, 1997).

At the heart of these questions is the extent to which PDSs have accepted conventional, apolitical views of equity. Conventional notions of equity generally equate it with equal access to resources and opportunity (Borunda & Murrell, 1996). Within this framework, children and their families are seen as clients to be served, treated, or fixed (Kendall, 1993; Pang, in press; Villegas, 1991). Schooling is viewed as a mechanism for equipping children with the skills they need to qualify for a share of a pie that somebody else has baked. This deficit model of education does not question whether the pie is particularly wholesome, nor does it regard children and their families as proper partners in deciding the issue (Borunda & Murrell, 1996; Lawson, 1996).

Although equal access is important, it is not necessarily sufficient to empower and enable historically marginalized groups to transform their own lives or the communities in which they live (Ayers, 1994; Borunda & Murrell, 1996; Valli, 1994). Because schools are a major socialization agent in most societies, they can perpetuate societal injustices and inequities, or they can help to eliminate them (Abdal-Haqq, 1994; Ayers, 1994). To perform the latter task requires teachers who possess an understanding of why and how marginalized students and their families become vulnerable, as well as competence in delivering instruction that informs, enables, and empowers (Lipman, 1997).

Isolated courses in multicultural education are unlikely to equip teachers for such work. Many such courses appear to take the "music appreciation" approach to diversity. They promote acceptance, tolerance, and even respect for diversity, but they do not necessarily affirm it (Nieto, 1992). They deliver generalizations about students' communities and cultures without probing beneath the surface of either construct. Escobar and Mukhopadhyay (1993) point out that culture is frequently and mistakenly equated with artifacts—the tangible, observable material products of culture—but in reality, both culture and community are complex, fluid, and dynamic concepts.

> Even the most ethnically homogenous neighborhood, is mi-
> croculturally, and hence, culturally diverse. . . . [E]thnicity
> constitutes only one type of microculture in which individuals
> participate; they are also involved in gender, religious, re-
> gional, national, occupational, organizational, and numerous
> other (including family) microcultures. Thus no ethnic com-
> munity is homogenous. Consequently, approaches to multi-
> cultural education that attempt to identify the learning style of
> Hispanics (or even Chicanas) or that try to provide student
> teachers with teaching strategies suitable for Asians, Hispan-
> ics, or African Americans, are inadequate. (p. 8)

PDS literature, as well as school change and diversity literature, cautions us about the limits of restructuring and teacher
change in bringing about meaningful improvements in students'
lives. Lipman's (1997) study of teacher participation in a restructuring initiative at a Southern junior high school demonstrated
"the limits of teacher participation and initiative without a con-
comitant challenge to existing structures of domination in the
school, district, and community" (p. 29). She found that new, empowering responsibilities and roles were given to teachers without
support for new thinking about the institutional and political roots
of students' attitudes, achievement levels, or behavior. Lipman
concluded that the restructuring experience raised important
questions about assumptions that empowering teachers facilitates
school-based change.

> Indeed, it brings into focus the absence of a necessary connec-
> tion between teacher participation and a process of teachers
> rethinking core assumptions about students and schooling.
> Although teacher involvement and professional collaboration
> may be indispensable, these new roles may not instigate a
> challenge to the politics of privilege so much at the center of
> the way schools work to reproduce inequity and disempower
> less privileged students—females, working-class students,
> children of color . . . If teacher participation is to make schools
> more liberatory, then it will need to be intimately linked with a
> critique of how dominant interests are played out in schools and
> how existing relations of domination are reproduced. (p. 33)

The focus of PDS activity thus far may be too narrow to achieve even the equity goals the movement has set for itself, let alone goals that reflect broader and deeper conceptions of equity. Both Borunda and Murrell (1996) and Lawson (1996) maintain that there may be inherent conceptual limitations on the prevailing PDS model's ability to bring about meaningful change in the lives of vulnerable, marginalized children and families. These authors suggest that alternate partnership concepts, which involve families and communities as partners in change, may be more efficacious. Lawson refers to second-generation partnerships that build upon the need for interprofessional practice and community collaboration.

These voices of caution emerge at a critical juncture in the PDS movement. Many partnerships are making strides toward institutionalizing the PDS in school districts and universities, with PDSs becoming the "accepted way of doing business" (Teitel, Reed, & O'Conner, 1997). Since 1995, the PDS Standards Project has engaged in a number of inquiry activities to inform its efforts to draft standards for PDSs (Levine, 1996b). These standards are intended to facilitate quality control and accountability and provide guidelines for development and implementation (Sykes, 1997).

This review of PDS literature confirms the pattern of uneven development within the movement that other authors have noted. The literature thus far is heavily tilted toward preservice and inservice teacher education; teaching and learning receive much less attention. A comparable imbalance is evident when we compare what the literature tells us about fulfilling commitments to parity and equity. Even judging by the conceptualization of equity that appears to have general acceptance within the movement, the PDS literature offers very little attention to issues of culturally relevant teaching.

If the literature accurately reflects the status of PDS development, we are therefore left with the impression that thus far, the majority of PDSs appear to serve primarily as more efficient delivery systems for educating teachers who continue to teach traditional subject matter in traditional fashion in traditional schools. Those who hoped for more enabling and empowering learning experiences for children are left to console themselves as best they can with the hope that the effects of more empowered, confident, and content teachers will trickle down to students. However, PDSs are schools, and like other schools, they may become equally resistant to change (Fullan, 1995). If, as Borunda and Murrell (1996) caution, the prevailing model and focus of PDSs assume a "hegemonic presence among school reform movements" (p. 4) and set the pattern for structuring working alliances between schools and colleges, what are the implications of such a monopoly for promoting collaborative efforts to address the learning and social needs of children and the ideological barriers to meeting those needs? It may be that meaningful standards can help unbalanced PDSs right themselves and give equal time to each aspect of their mission.

In the absence of some significant realignment, PDS supporters like Teitel, Reed, and O'Conner (1997) are forced to raise the question of exactly what is being institutionalized. W. E. B. DuBois cautioned African Americans more than 50 years ago not to be so anxious to get a seat on the train that they do not stop to question where the train is going. PDS implementers might well heed such advice before embracing the comforts of becoming a line item in somebody's annual budget.

References

Abdal-Haqq, I. (1991). *Professional development schools and education reform: Concepts and concerns*. ERIC Digest 91-2. Washington, DC: ERIC Clearinghouse on Teaching and Teacher Education.

Abdal-Haqq, I. (1994). *Culturally responsive curriculum*. ERIC Digest 93-5. Washington, DC: ERIC Clearinghouse on Teaching and Teacher Education.

Abdal-Haqq, I. (1995a). *Infusing technology into preservice teacher education*. ERIC Digest 94-6. Washington, DC: ERIC Clearinghouse on Teaching and Teacher Education.

Abdal-Haqq, I. (Comp.). (1995b). *Professional development schools: A directory of projects in the United States* (2nd ed.). Washington, DC: American Association of Colleges for Teacher Education.

Abdal-Haqq, I. (1996a). An information provider's perspective on the professional development school movement. *Contemporary Education, 67*(4), 237-240.

Abdal-Haqq, I. (1996b). *Making time for teacher professional development*. ERIC Digest 95-4. Washington, DC: ERIC Clearinghouse on Teaching and Teacher Education.

Abdal-Haqq, I. (in press). *Preparing teachers for urban schools: A report on the Teachers for Tomorrow program*. Washington, DC: American Association of Colleges for Teacher Education.

Alber, S. (1995, April). *Meeting the challenge for high level parental involvement in an urban professional development school*. Paper presented at the Association of Teacher Educators Summer Conference, Williamsburg, VA.

American Association of Colleges for Teacher Education (AACTE). (1995). *RATE VIII: Teaching teachers—Relationships with the world of practice*. Washington, DC: Author.

Anderson, R. (Ed.). (1993). *Voices of change: A report of the Clinical Schools Project*. Washington, DC: American Association of Colleges for Teacher Education.

Anderson, M., Boles, K., Abascal, J., Barand, M. D., Bourne, L., Brown, J., Cassidy, M. B., & Holzapfel, D. (1995, April). *The reflective mentoring seminar: Providing means for teachers to cross boundaries in a professional development school.* Paper presented at the annual meeting of the American Educational Research Association, San Francisco.

Arends, R., & Winitzky, N. (1996). Program structures and learning to teach. In F. B. Murray (Ed.), *The teacher educator's handbook: Building a knowledge base for the preparation of teachers* (pp. 526-556). San Francisco: Jossey-Bass.

Ariav, T., & Clinard, L. M. (1996, July). *Does coaching student teachers affect the professional development and teaching of cooperating teachers? A cross-cultural perspective.* Paper presented at the Second International Conference of the Mofet Institute, Israel.

Ayers, W. (1994). Skin-game: Race and racism in teaching and teacher education. In J. M. Novak (Ed.), *Democratic teacher education* (pp. 215-28). Albany: State University of New York Press.

Barba, R., Seideman, I., Schneider, H., & Mera, M. (1993). *School of Education Secondary Teacher Education Program. Professional Development Schools Project. Status report.* Unpublished manuscript. School of Education, University of Massachusetts, Amherst.

Bell, N. M. (1995). *Professional development sites: Revitalizing preservice education in middle schools.* (ERIC Document Reproduction Service No. ED382583)

Berry, B., Boles, K., Edens, K., Nissenholtz, A., & Trachtman, R. (1996). *Inquiry in professional development schools.* Unpublished manuscript. National Center for Restructuring Education, Schools, and Teaching, Teachers College, Columbia University, New York.

Boles, K., & Troen, V. (1994). *Teacher leadership in a professional development school.* Paper presented at the annual meeting of the American Educational Research Association, New Orleans.

Book, C. L. (1996). Professional development schools. In J. Sikula, T. J. Buttery, & E. Guyton (Eds.), *Handbook of research on teacher education* (2nd ed., pp. 194-210). New York: Simon & Schuster Macmillan.

Borunda, M. R., & Murrell, Jr., P. C. (1996) *What's missing in professional development schools: Cultural politics of educational equity in PDSs.* Unpublished draft manuscript. National Center for Restructuring Education, Schools, and Teaching, Teachers College, Columbia University, New York.

Bucci, J. A., & Reitzammer, A. F. (1992). Collaboration with health and social services professionals: Preparing teachers for new roles. *Journal of Teacher Education, 43,* 290-295.

Bullough, Jr., R. V., Kauchak, D., Crow, N., Hobbs, S., & Stokes, D. (1997a). Long-term PDS development in research universities and the clinicalization of teacher education. *Journal of Teacher Education, 48,* 85-95.

Bullough, Jr., R. V., Kauchak, D., Crow, N., Hobbs, S., & Stokes, D. (1997b). Professional development schools: Catalysts for teacher and school change. *Teaching and Teacher Education, 13*(2): 153-171.

Buttery, T. J., & Anderson, P. J. (1997, February). *Community, school, and parent dynamics: A synthesis of literature and activities.* Paper presented at the annual conference of the Association of Teacher Educators, Washington, DC.

Campbell, T. A., Strawderman, C., & Reavis, C.A. (1996). Professional development schools: Collaboration and change. *Teacher Education Quarterly, 3*(2), 94.

Carey, N., & Farris, E. (1996). *Parents and schools: Partners in student learning.* Statistics in Brief NCES 96-913. Washington, DC: U.S. Department of Education.

Carnegie Forum on Education and the Economy. (1986). *A nation prepared: Teachers for the 21st century.* Washington, DC: Author.

Center for Educational Renewal. (1995, December). Leadership Associates' inquiry projects cover many topics. *Center Correspondent.* (Available from Center for Educational Renewal, Miller Hall DQ-12, University of Washington, Seattle, WA 98195)

Century Communications. (1996). *The Students as Authors Project.* [Videocassette]. Morgantown, West Virginia: Author. (Available from Students as Authors Project, Central Elementary School, Morgantown, WV 26505-5601)

Chase, S., Merryfield, M., & Chism, E. (1996, April). *Bridging the gap between campus and school through collaboration in a professional development school network in social studies and global education.* Paper presented at the annual meeting of the American Educational Research Association, New York.

Clark, R. W. (1995). Evaluating partner schools. In R. T. Osguthorpe, R. C. Harris, M. F. Harris, & S. Black (Eds.), *Partner schools: Centers for educational renewal* (pp. 229-262). San Francisco: Jossey-Bass.

Clark, R. W. (1997). *Professional development schools: Policy and financing. A guide for policymakers.* Washington, DC: American Association of Colleges for Teacher Education.

Clark, R. W., & Plecki, M. L. (1997). Professional development schools: Their costs and financing. In M. Levine & R. Trachtman (Eds.), *Making professional development schools work: Politics, practices, and policy* (pp. 134-158). New York: Teachers College Press.

Collinson, V., Hohenbrink, J., Sherrill, J., & Bible, R. (1994). *Changing contexts for changing roles: Teachers as learners and leaders in universities, professional development schools, and school districts.* Paper presented at the annual conference of the Association for Supervision and Curriculum Development, Chicago.

Conroy, M. C., Jensen, L. C., Bainbridge, & Catron, R. (1996). Enhancing teacher education through collaboration: The electronic highway connects college and partner schools. In T. Warren (Ed.), *Partnerships in teacher education* (pp. 27-41). Lanham, MD: University Press of America.

A conversation with Dr. Linda Darling-Hammond. (1997, Spring). *Resources for Restructuring.* Newsletter of the National Center for Restructuring Education, Schools, and Teaching. (Available from NCREST, Box 110, Teachers College, Columbia University, New York, NY 10027)

Crawford, S., Smith, P. G., Thacker, D., Turner, M. C., & Watkins, S. (1993). Building a school-university relationship: The emerging roles of clinical professors. *Contemporary Education, 64,* 255-257.

Crow, N., Stokes, D., Kauchak, D., Hobbs, S., & Bullough, Jr., R. V. (1996, April). *Masters cooperative program: An alternative model of teacher development in PDS sites.* Paper presented at the annual meeting of the American Educational Research Association, New York.

Cummins, J., & Sayers, D. (1995). *Brave new schools: Challenging cultural illiteracy through global learning networks.* New York: St. Martin's.

Darling-Hammond, L. (1994). Developing professional development schools: Early lessons, challenges, and promises. In L. Darling-Hammond (Ed.), *Professional development schools: Schools for developing a profession* (pp. 1-27). New York: Teachers College Press.

Dempsey, V. (1997). The nature of professionalism in the context of school reform. In N. E. Hoffman, W. M. Reed, & G. S. Rosenbluth (Eds.), *Lessons from restructuring experiences: Stories of change in professional development schools* (pp. 9-32). Albany: State University of New York Press.

Devlin-Scherer, R. (1993). Learning to teach in the inner city and with diverse populations: A professional development school model with accountability. *Contemporary Education, 64,* 230-233.

DeWert, M. H., & Cory, S. L. (1996). Becoming partners: Building a school/university collaboration focused on teaching and learning with technology. *Journal of Computing in Teacher Education, 12*(3), 8-12.

Duquette, C., & Cook, S. A. (1994). Five Ontario professional development schools. *Journal of Professional Studies, 1*(2), 60-72.

Escobar, D., & Mukhopadhyay, C. (1993). Communities within communities. In M. Guy (Ed.), *Teachers and teacher education: Essays on the national education goals* (pp. 1-20). Washington, DC: ERIC Clearinghouse on Teacher Education.

Fishbaugh, M. S. E., & Rose, E. (1997). Montana State University—Billings professional development school. In R. D. Benton (Ed.), *Partnerships for learning: Real issues and real solutions* (pp. 46-49). Oshkosh, WI: Teacher Education Council of State Colleges and Universities.

Fountain, C., & Evans, D. (1994). Beyond shared rhetoric: A collaborative change model for integrating preservice and inservice urban educational delivery systems. *Journal of Teacher Education, 45*, 218-228.

Four Cities Urban PDS Network. (1995, Spring). Newsletter of the Four Cities Urban Professional Development School Network. (Available from Center for Teacher Education, University of Wisconsin—Milwaukee, P.O. Box 413, Milwaukee, WI 53201)

Fullan, M. (1995). Contexts: Overview and framework. In M. J. O'Hair & S. Odell (Eds.), *Educating teachers for leadership and change. Teacher Education Yearbook III* (pp. 1-10). Thousand Oaks, CA: Corwin.

Gardner, W. E., & Libde, A. A. (1995). Professional development schools: How well do they travel? *Journal of Education for Teaching, 21*, 303-316.

Goodlad, J. (1990). *Teachers for our nation's schools.* San Francisco: Jossey-Bass.

Gottesman, B., Graham, P., & Nogy, C. (1993). *South Carolina Center for the Advancement of Teaching and School Leadership: Professional development schools.* Rock Hill: South Carolina Center for the Advancement of Teaching and School Leadership, Winthrop College.

Hausfather, S. J., Outlaw, M. E., & Strehle, E. L. (1996). Relationships as a foundation: Emerging field experiences within multiple college-school partnerships. In T. Warren (Ed.), *Partnerships in teacher education* (pp. 27-41). Lanham, MD: University Press of America.

Hayes, H. A., & Wetherill, K. S. (1996, April). *A new vision for schools, supervision, and teacher education: The professional development system and Model Clinical Teaching Project.* Paper presented at the annual meeting of the American Educational Research Association, New York.

Hecht, J. B., Bland, S. J., Schoon, P. L., & Boschert, K. (1996). *Professional development schools 1995-96. A research report.* Normal: Illinois State University, College of Education, Technological Innovations in Educational Research Laboratory.

Hoffman, N. E., Reed, W. M., & Rosenbluth, G. S. (1997). Introduction. In N. E. Hoffman, W. M. Reed, & G. S. Rosenbluth (Eds.), *Lessons from restructuring experiences: Stories of change in professional development schools* (pp. 1-6). Albany: State University of New York Press.

Holmes Group. (1986). *Tomorrow's teachers.* East Lansing, MI: Author.

Holmes Group. (1990). *Tomorrow's schools: Principles for the design of professional development schools.* East Lansing, MI: Author.

Holmes Group. (1995). *Tomorrow's schools of education.* East Lansing, MI: Author.

Hopkins, W. S., Hoffman, S. Q., & Moss, V. D. (1997). Professional development schools and preservice teacher stress. *Action in Teacher Education, 18*(4), 36-46.

Houston, W. R., Clay, D., Hollis, L. Y., Ligons, C., Roff, L., & Lopez, N. (1995). *Strength through diversity: Houston Consortium for Professional*

Development and Technology Centers. Houston, TX: University of Houston, College of Education.

Houston Consortium of Professional Development. (1996, April). *ATE Newsletter*, p. 7.

Ishler, R., & Edens, K. (1995). *Professional development schools: What are they? What are the issues and challenges? How are they funded? How should they be evaluated?* Kingston, RI: Association of Colleges and Schools of Education in State Universities and Land Grant Colleges and Affiliated Private Universities.

Jett-Simpson, M., Pugach, M. C., & Whipp, J. (1992, April). *Portrait of an urban professional development school*. Paper presented at the annual meeting of the American Educational Research Association, San Francisco.

Judge, H., Carriedo, R., & Johnson, S. M. (1995). *Professional development schools and MSU. The report of the 1995 review* [On-line]. Available: http://35.8.168.203/kiosk/PDS_Rpt.html

Kendall, E. D. (1993). Family and school coalitions: Surmounting obstacles. In M. Guy (Ed.), *Teachers and teacher education: Essays on the national education goals* (Teacher Education Monograph No. 16, pp. 21-34). Washington, DC: ERIC Clearinghouse on Teacher Education, American Association of Colleges for Teacher Education.

King, Jr., A., & Mizoue, Y. (1993). A case for university-based professional development and experimental schools: Japanese and American perspectives. *Peabody Journal of Education, 68*(3), 67-79.

Kleinsasser, A. M., & Paradis, E. E. (1997). Changing teacher education in the context of a school-university partnership: Disrupting temporal organizational arrangements. *Teacher Education Quarterly, 24*(2), 63-73.

Kozleski, E. B., Anderson-Parsons, B., Foster, A., Mantle-Bromley, C., Walters, B., & Wilson, C. (1997). *Evaluating partnerships: A robust approach to improving partnerships*. In R. D. Benton (Ed.), *Partnerships for learning: Real issues and real solutions* (pp. 186-198). Oshkosh, WI: Teacher Education Council of State Colleges and Universities.

Lancy, R. (1997). The Thomas Jefferson Professional Development School. In M. Levine & R. Trachtman (Eds.), *Making professional development schools work: Politics, practices, and policy* (pp. 215-233). New York: Teachers College Press.

Lange, D. L. (1993). Professional development schools and teacher education. In M. Guy (Ed.), *Teachers and teacher education: Essays on the national education goals*. Washington, DC: ERIC Clearinghouse on Teaching and Teacher Education.

Lawrence, S. M. (1997). Beyond race awareness: White racial identity and multicultural teaching. *Journal of Teacher Education, 48*, 108-117.

Lawson, H. A. (1996). Expanding the Goodlad agenda: Interprofessional education and community collaboration in service of vulnerable children, youth, and families. *Holistic Education Review, 9*(1), 20-34.

Lawson, H. A., Flora, R., Lloyd, S., Briar, K., Ziegler, & Kettlewell, J. (1995). Building links with families and communities. In R. T. Osguthorpe, R. C. Harris, M. F. Harris, & S. Black (Eds.), *Partner schools: Centers for educational renewal* (pp. 205-228). San Francisco: Jossey-Bass.

LeCompe, K., Irby, B. J., & Lara-Alecio, R. (1995). *Community learning: A field-based education model.* (ERIC Document Reproduction Service No. ED399222)

Lemlech, J. K., Hertzog-Foliart, H., & Hackl, A. (1994). The Los Angeles professional practice school. In L. Darling-Hammond (Ed.), *Professional development schools: Schools for developing a profession* (pp. 156-175). New York: Teachers College Press.

Levine, M. (Ed.). (1988). *Professional practice schools: Building a model. Vol. 1.* Washington, DC: American Federation of Teachers.

Levine, M. (1992). Introduction. In M. Levine (Ed.), *Professional practice schools: Linking teacher education and school reform* (pp. 1-7). New York: Teachers College Press.

Levine, M. (1996a). Educating teachers for restructured schools. In F. Murray (Ed.), *The teacher educator's handbook: Building a knowledge base for the preparation of teachers* (pp. 620-647). San Francisco: Jossey-Bass.

Levine, M. (1996b). *Professional development school standards project synthesis paper. A work in progress.* Unpublished manuscript. National Council for the Accreditation of Teacher Education (NCATE), Professional Development School Standards Project, Washington, DC.

Lieberman, A., & Miller, L. (1992). Teacher development in professional practice schools. In M. Levine (Ed.), *Professional practice schools: Linking teacher education and school reform* (pp. 105-123). New York: Teachers College Press.

Lipman, P. (1997). Restructuring in context: A case study of teacher participation and the dynamics of ideology, race, and power. *American Educational Research Journal, 34*(1), 3-38.

Long, J. (1996). *Research analysis of professional development school graduates.* Unpublished manuscript. The Teachers College of Emporia State University, Emporia, KS.

Lyons, N. (1996). A grassroots experiment in performance assessment. *Educational Leadership, 53*(6), 64-67.

Martin, D. (1996). *Project Achieve: 24 month progress report.* Washington, DC: Department of Education, Gallaudet University.

Maryland Higher Education Commission. (1995). *Teacher Education Task Force report.* Baltimore, MD: Author.

McLaughlin, M. W. (1994). Somebody knows my name. In *Issues in Restructuring Schools* (Issue Report No. 7, pp. 9-11). Madison, WI: University of Wisconsin—Madison, Center on Organization and Restructuring of Schools.

Meyers, C. (1996, April). *Beyond PDSs: Schools as professional learning communities: A proposal based on an analysis of PDS efforts of the 1990's*. Paper presented at the annual meeting of the American Educational Research Association, New York.

Michigan State University. (1995, May). *Professional development schools* [Online]. (Program transcript, Michigan Gateways No. 307). Available: http://web.msu.edu/comptech/gateways/307trn.html

Miller, L., & O'Shea, C. (1994). *Partnership: Getting broader, getting deeper. NCREST reprint series*. New York: National Center for Restructuring Education, Schools, and Teaching, Teachers College, Columbia University, New York.

Minnesota State Board of Teaching. (1994). *Developing a residency program as part of teacher licensure*. St. Paul, MN: Author.

The Model Clinical Teaching Program. (n.d.). (Available from Model Clinical Teaching Program, School of Education, East Carolina University, Greenville, NC 27858)

Morris, V. G., & Nunnery, J. A. (1993). *Teacher empowerment in a professional development school collaborative: Pilot assessment* (Technical Report 931101). Memphis, TN: Memphis State University, Center for Research in Educational Policy, College of Education.

Morse, S., Daniels, T., & Flieg, F. (1995, February). *An early childhood professional development school: Triumphs and troubles*. Paper presented at the annual meeting of the American Association of Colleges for Teacher Education, Washington, DC.

Murray, F. B. (1993). "All or none" criteria for professional development schools. *Educational Policy, 7*(1), 61-73.

National Center for Restructuring Education, Schools, and Teaching (NCREST). (1995). *Preparing teachers for learner centered practice: The professional development school at PS 87* [Videocassette]. NCREST, Teachers College, Columbia University, New York.

National Center for Restructuring Education, Schools, and Teaching (NCREST). (1996). *The lightning post-office* [Videocassette]. NCREST, Teachers College, Columbia University, New York.

National Commission on Teaching and America's Future. (1996). *What matters most: Teaching for America's future*. New York: Author.

National Education Commission on Time and Learning (NECTL). (1994). *Prisoners of time*. Washington, DC: Author. (ERIC Document Reproduction Service No. ED366115)

National PTA. (1997). *National standards for parent/family involvement programs* [On-line]. Available: http://www.pta.org/programs/stnrdtoc.html

Neufeld, J. A., & McGowan, T. M. (1993). Professional development schools: A witness to teacher empowerment. *Contemporary Education, 64,* 249-251.

Newman, C., Moss, B., Naher-Snoeden, J., Hruschak, L., Kovack, J., & Pangas, C. (1996, October). *Transforming teacher education, teaching and student learning in a professional development school collaborative: A work in progress.* Paper presented at the annual meeting of the Midwestern Educational Research Association, Chicago.

Nieto, S. (1992). *Affirming diversity: The sociocultural context of multicultural education.* White Plains, NY: Longman.

Office of Technology Assessment. (1995). *Teachers and technology: Making the connection. OTA report summary.* Washington, DC: U.S. Government Printing Office.

Osguthorpe, R. T., Harris, R. C., Harris, M. F., & Black, S. (1995). Appendix: National Network for Educational Renewal site descriptions. In R. T. Osguthorpe, R. C. Harris, M. F. Harris, & S. Black (Eds.), *Partner schools: Centers for educational renewal* (pp. 283-310). San Francisco: Jossey-Bass.

Pang, V. O. (in press). Teacher efficacy: How do teachers feel about their ability to teach African-American students? In M. E. Dilworth (Ed.), *Considerations of culture in teacher education: An anthology on practice.* Thousand Oaks, CA: Corwin.

Papoulia-Tzelepi, P. (1993). Teaching practice curriculum in teacher education. *European Journal of Teacher Education, 16,* 147-162.

Pasch, S. H., & Pugach, M. C. (1990). Collaborative planning for urban professional development schools. *Contemporary Education, 61*(3), 135-43.

PDS Proceedings. (1996, Fall). Newsletter of the University of South Carolina Professional Development Schools Network. (Available from PDS Network, 102 Wardlaw, University of South Carolina, Columbia, SC 29208)

Pechman, E. (1992). The child as meaning maker: The organizing principle for professional practice shools. In M. Levine (Ed.), *Professional practice schools: Linking teacher education and school reform* (pp. 25-62). New York: Teachers College Press.

Persichitte, K., Tharp, D., & Caffarella, E. (1997, February). *The use of technology by schools, colleges, and departments of education: Fall, 1996.* Paper presented at the annual meeting of the American Association of Colleges for Teacher Education, Phoenix, AZ.

Petrie, H. G. (Ed.). (1995). *Professionalization, partnership, and power: Building professional development schools.* Albany: State University of New York Press.

The professional development community. (1994, May). Unpublished project description. (Available from Center for Collaborative Advancement of the Teaching Profession, School of Education, University of Louisville, Louisville, KY 40292)

Professional development school programs in serious emotional disturbance at Marshall Road Center and Pathways/Hyattsville. (n.d.). Unpublished project description. (Available from Department of Teacher Education, George Washington University, Washington, DC)

Radner, B., Griego, I., & Wiener, B. (1994, April). Metropolitan State College of Denver. *Center Correspondent.* Newsletter of the Center for Educational Renewal. (Available from Center for Educational Renewal, Miller Hall DQ-12, University of Washington, Seattle, WA 98195)

Rasch, K., & Finch, M. E. (1996). Who are our partners? Reconceptualizing teaching and stewardship. In T. Warren (Ed.), *Partnerships in teacher education* (pp. 135-142). Lanham, MD: University Press of America.

Saab, J. F., Steel, S., & Shive, J. (1997). Teachers' perspectives on school change. In N. E. Hoffman, W. M. Reed, & G. S. Rosenbluth (Eds.), *Lessons from restructuring experiences: Stories of change in professional development schools* (pp. 245-268). Albany: State University of New York Press.

Sandoval, P. A., Reed, C., & Attinasi, J. (1993). Professors and teachers working together to develop instructional teams in an urban teacher education program. *Contemporary Education, 64,* 243-248.

Scannell, D. (1996). Evaluating professional development schools: The challenge of an imperative. *Journal of Teacher Education, 67,* 241-243.

School-linked comprehensive services for children and families. What we know and what we need to know (Rep. No. SAI-95-3025). (1995). Washington, DC: U.S. Department of Education, Office of Educational Research and Improvement.

Shive, J. (1997). Collaboration between K-12 schools and universities. In N. E. Hoffman, W. M. Reed, & G. S. Rosenbluth (Eds.), *Lessons from restructuring experiences: Stories of change in professional development schools* (pp. 33-50). Albany: State University of New York Press.

Stallings, J. A., & Kowalski, T. (1990). Research on professional development schools. In W. R. Houston, M. Haberman, & J. Sikula (Eds.), *Handbook of research on teacher education* (pp. 251-263). New York: Macmillan.

Swanson, J. (1995). *Systemic reform in the professionalism of educators. Vol. I: Findings and conclusions. Studies of education reform.* (ERIC Document Reproduction Service No. ED397556)

Sykes, G. (1997). Worthy of the name: Standards for professional development schools. In M. Levine & R. Trachtman (Eds.), *Making professional development schools work: Politics, practices, and policy* (pp. 159-184). New York: Teachers College Press.

Task force on the role and future of minorities: American Educational Research Association. (1997). *Educational Researcher, 26*(3), 44-52.

Teitel, L. (1993). The state role in jump-starting school/university collaboration: A case study. *Educational Policy, 7*(1), 74-95.

Teitel, L. (1996). *Professional development schools: A literature review.* Unpublished manuscript. (Available from Professional Development School Standards Project, National Council for Accreditation of Teacher Education, Washington, DC 20036)

Teitel, L. (1997a). The organization and governance of professional development schools. In M. Levine & R. Trachtman (Eds.), *Making professional development schools work: Politics, practices, and policy* (pp. 115-133). New York: Teachers College Press.

Teitel, L. (1997b). Professional development schools and the transformation of teacher leadership. *Teacher Education Quarterly, 24*(1), 9-22.

Teitel, L., Reed, C., & O'Conner, K. (Eds.). (1997). *Institutionalizing professional development schools.* Unpublished manuscript. National Center for Restructuring Education, Schools, and Teaching, Teachers College, Columbia University, New York.

Trachtman, R. (1996). *The NCATE professional development school study: A survey of 28 PDS sites.* Unpublished manuscript. (Available from Professional Development School Standards Project, National Council for Accreditation of Teacher Education, Washington, DC 20036)

Troen, V., & Boles, K. (1994). Two teachers examine the power of teacher leadership. In D. R. Walling (Ed.), *Teachers as leaders. Perspectives on the professional development of teachers* (pp. 275-286), Bloomington, IN: Phi Delta Kappa Educational Foundation.

Tusin, L. (1995, February). *Success in the first year of teaching: Effects of a clinical experience program.* Paper presented at the annual meeting of the Association of Teacher Educators, Detroit, MI.

Type 2. (1996, Fall). Newsletter of the National Network of Partnership—2000 Schools. (Available from National Network of Partnership—2000 Schools, Johns Hopkins University, 3505 North Charles Street, Baltimore, MD 21218)

U.S. Department of Education, Partnership for Family Involvement in Education. (n.d.) *America goes back to school. Partners' activity kit 1996-97.* Washington, DC: Author.

Valli, L. (1994, April). *Professional development schools: An opportunity to reconceptualize schools and teacher education as empowering learning communities.* Paper presented at the International Seminar on Teacher Education (ISTE) annual meeting, Maastricht, Netherlands.

Valli, L., Cooper, D., & Frankes, L. (1997). Professional development schools and equity: A critical analysis of rhetoric and research. In M. W. Apple (Ed.), *Review of research in education 22* (pp. 251-304). Washington, DC: American Educational Research Association.

Vaughn, A. J. (1996). *School renewal and non-instructional time for teachers: Profiles from the National Network for Educational Renewal* (Reflections on Practice Series No. 1). Seattle: University of Washington, Center for Educational Renewal.

Villegas, A. M. (1991). *Culturally responsive pedagogy for the 1990s and beyond* (Trends and Issues Paper No. 6). Washington, DC: ERIC Clearinghouse on Teacher Education.

Vision statement: Professional Development Schools Network. (1993, October). *PDS Network News.* Newsletter of the Professional Development Schools Network. (Available from NCREST Box 110, Teachers College, Columbia University, New York, NY 10027)

Warner, A. R. (1996). Funding field-based, technology-intensive professional preparation. *Teacher Education and Practice, 12*(1), 41-46.

Watts, G. D., & Castle, S. (1993). The time dilemma in school restructuring. *Phi Delta Kappan, 75*(4), 306-310.

Webb-Dempsey, J. (n.d.). *Benedum Collaborative professional development schools. Impact assessment study. Initial findings from student data collection pilot in the five original PDS sites.* Draft. Unpublished manuscript. West Virginia University, College of Human Resources and Education, Center for the Renewal of Professional Preparation and Practice, Morgantown.

Webb-Dempsey, J. (1997). Reconsidering assessment to be reflective of school reform. In N. E. Hoffman, W. M. Reed, & G. S. Rosenbluth (Eds.), *Lessons from restructuring experiences: Stories of change in professional development schools* (pp. 269-294). Albany: State University of New York Press.

Whitford, B. L. (1994). Permission, persistence, and resistance: Linking high school restructuring with teacher education reform. In L. Darling-Hammond (Ed.), *Professional development schools: Schools for developing a profession* (pp. 74-97). New York: Teachers College Press.

Williams, R. O. (1996). Professional development schools: Facing the challenge of institutionalization. *Contemporary Education, 67,* 171-179.

Wiseman, D. L., & Cooner, D. (1996). Discovering the power of collaboration: The impact of a school-university partnership on teaching. *Teacher Education and Practice, 12*(1), 18-28.

Zeichner, K. (1992). Rethinking the practicum in the professional development school partnership. *Journal of Teacher Education, 43,* 296-307.

Zeichner, K., & Miller, M. (1997). Learning to teach in professional development schools. In M. Levine & R. Trachtman (Eds.), *Making professional development schools work: Politics, practices, and policy* (pp. 15-32). New York: Teachers College Press.

Index

CORWIN
PRESS

The Corwin Press logo—a raven striding across an open book
—represents the happy union of courage and learning. We are a
professional-level publisher of books and journals for K–12 educators, and we are committed to creating and providing resources
that embody these qualities. Corwin's motto is "Success for All
Learners."